The Tri-Tribulation Rapture Of The Church

1335 THE KEY
Dan. 12:12

Robert L. Dickey, PhD

Kingdom Advance Publishing
P. O. Box 48288
Los Angeles, California 90048
877.333.5075

www.robertandaudreydickeyministries.org

Printed in the United States of America

ISBN: 978-0-9997611-0-6

Library of Congress Control Number: 2017919526
Kingdom Advance Publishing, Los Angeles, CA

Cover design by Robert L. Dickey, PhD

Christian Theology/Eschatology
Biblical Studies/Prophecy

To Audrey M'love, my wife forever, whom God gave to me. To my children, grandchildren, believers (both Christian and Jewish) and to non-believers everywhere who want to know End-Time truth. May you be blessed by the revelation I received from God regarding the Tri-Tribulation Rapture of the Church.

CONTENTS

FORWARD

The Bible says, if you read the book of Revelation, you will be blessed (Revelation 1:3). Yet many shy away from doing so, from laymen to Pastors and spiritual leaders.

I have found reading the book of Revelation and receiving the fullness of the mysteries God has allowed to be uncovered, requires a *gift* of prophecy from God Himself.

My faithful husband, Dr. Robert, is one of the best End-Time Bible Prophecy teachers I have heard. The Lord has blessed him to uncover a gigantic mystery that will bring so much revelation, comfort, and peace to the Body of Christ, His Kingdom. All those searching for truth regarding the End-Times we live in and beyond will certainly find answers in these pages.

Dr. Robert not only has uncovered mysteries, but God has given him insight to accurately calculate the signs of the times we now face. Revealing the Tri-Tribulation Rapture of the Church will be an experience that encompasses all three raptures and what they will mean to millions of souls, which is nothing short of a miracle and a blessing.

When Dr. Robert first explained to me what he discovered, I was intrigued. Personally, in my nearly thirty years in ministry, I had not heard it explained this way. I am not an end-times bible minister, but I am aware of the subject and its complications throughout the years, being a student of the Word myself.

Dr. Robert has successfully drawn together three amazing conclusions that work with scripture and all three viewpoints of the Rapture. Not many are aware that a battle has been raging for years between Bible scholars and teachers regarding the following three views:

The Pre-Tribulation Rapture

The Mid-Tribulation Rapture

The Post-Tribulation Rapture

The confusion can end because whoever reads this material will be blessed to see how he breaks down the three arguments. I am so grateful for what God has revealed to Dr. Robert and what God plans for His children. He has made provision for all that come to Him; none will be left behind because they missed the first or even the second rapture. Because of His grace and mercy, they will have the opportunity for a third rapture.

To God be the glory, now and forever!!!

Audrey L. Dickey, PhD

Co-Founder of Christian Love Glory International Center home of, Christian Love Fellowship Church, Inc. and Marketplace Businesses in Los Angeles, California.

PREFACE

It is the glory of God to conceal a matter, but the glory of kings is to search out a matter. Proverbs 25:2

After reading through the Bible several times, as well as reading and listening to various theories on the Rapture, it became increasingly clear each theory could not make an airtight defense of its viewpoint. Through interpretation and exegesis (explanation) of scriptures that support a particular viewpoint, a strong case for the Rapture can be made. However, I found with each theory there were scriptures that would or could definitely point to a different conclusion as to when the Rapture could or might occur.

I would like to thank at this point, Dr Melinda Michaelson Thomas President of Friends International Christian University, the faculty and Dr Kevin Thomas my advisor for encouraging me and assisting me with my doctoral thesis *The Rapture/Catching Away of the Church: Is it one event or three events: Pre-Tribulation; Mid-Tribulation and Post-Tribulation in order to completely remove all Believers from the Earth before Armageddon?* This book is an outgrowth of that dissertation more condensed and readable.

As I pondered the question for myself, I chose to receive the view of the Pre-Tribulation *theologians* that the Rapture would occur before the peace treaty of Daniel 9:27

is signed. Why not? Who would deliberately choose to go through the worst tribulation the world would ever experience? However, I could not shake the fact the other major viewpoints could make a case for their particular viewpoint to the exclusion of the Pre-Tribulation viewpoint. As an avid viewer of the Trinity Broadcasting Network, I would hear the late Paul Crouch repeatedly say he was "going on the first load, " referring to the fact, for him, Pre-Tribulation was the best viewpoint to choose.

So, when you consider the following: The Bible is the inerrant truth of God (John 17:17); God is not a man and cannot lie (Numbers 23:19); and God knows the end from the beginning (Isaiah 46:10); you have to conclude there has to be an explanation to satisfy all scriptures regarding the Rapture.

When you consider the Bible is a prophetic document that has accurately recorded future events throughout recorded history, you must give serious consideration to any prophesied event mentioned in it and take it seriously. Jesus Christ/Yeshua HaMashiach spoke of several events that shall take place and allude to a rapture event. Paul, the writer of most of the New Testament, writes what is, for most, if not all, the premier scripture regarding the Rapture in 1 Thessalonians 4:13-17.

For those who may say there are contradictions in the Bible regarding the Rapture, I say NO! There are only errors in interpretation by us, theologians, apostles, and prophets who try to give their own interpretation of what God has said. Even the Apostle Peter said the Apostle Paul spoke of some things which were hard to understand (2 Peter 3:16). Apostle Paul fully believed the Rapture he prophesied about would take place in his lifetime (1 Thessalonians 1:10).

However, according to Revelation 5:10, we have been made "kings and priests to our God"; therefore, according to Proverbs 25:2, we as kings and priests of God must search out this matter of the Rapture of the church. As we search the scriptures, we can give our best projection as to what God said regarding the Rapture. In the end, we shall know what the truth is. Until then, we give our best revelation as to what is to come.

What follows is my best revelation regarding the Rapture of the church. I have attempted to present the subject of the Rapture in a form that is clear so those who are novices can understand it as well as those who are well-informed. For the novice, he or she that is not versed or familiar with rapture theory, would do well to read the entire book. For those who know rapture theory might go to Chapter Seven *My Reconciliation of the Tri-Tribulation Rapture.*

I pray the reader is blessed by this revelation of *The Tri-Tribulation Rapture of The Church.*

LIST OF TABLES

INTRODUCTION

There are many popular theories regarding the *Rapture*. However, none has proved to be satisfactory for me, for the following reasons:

- According to Hebrews 13:8, "Jesus Christ is the same yesterday, today and forever." Therefore, Jesus would not have a Rapture in the Old Testament (Genesis 5:24, 2 Kings 2:11) and not in the New Testament as 2 Corinthians 12:2 and in the book of Revelation 4:2; 7:14; 14:14-16 attest to.

- God is not the author of confusion (1 Corinthians 14:33). Therefore, when we properly recognize what the Word of God is saying, all scripture should agree and not be in opposition to other scripture causing strife and confusion.

- Each theory or viewpoint leaves out scriptures pertaining to the rapture in order to make their viewpoint represent the soundest view.

- The *this is the only way it shall occur* viewpoint promotes fear rather than to comfort us as scripture tells us in 1 Thessalonians 4:17-18:

    Then we who are alive and remain shall be shall be caught up together with them in the clouds to meet the Lord in the air. And thus, we shall always be with the Lord. Therefore comfort one another with these words.

I am not suggesting having more than one opportunity and not just one instance of the rapture occurring is unique. There have been others. However, it is generally taken there will be only one instance in time when the Lord Jesus Christ/Yeshua HaMashiach will take the living and the dead believers out of this world before, during or after a time of the greatest distress the world has ever known (1 Corinthians 15:51-52, Matthew 24:21). This then is the motivation for the need of reconciliation of the different views regarding the Rapture of the Church.

After an in-depth search of the literature on the subject of the Rapture, I have presented a representative viewpoint for each of the three major theories: Pre-Tribulation Rapture, Mid-Tribulation Rapture, and the Post-Tribulation Rapture. I will give an overview of each theory. The explanation will give a good understanding of each. My premise is the Holy Bible, whether Old or New Testament, is true. The primary text used for this exposition (account) will be the New King James Version (NKJV).

What has come as a revelation to me is a biblical, objective and logical explanation can tie each of these positions together. Therefore, the three main views joined into one unified view, having clarity and purpose allows the Body of Christ to be on one accord regarding the Tri-Tribulation Rapture of the church.

It is not my purpose to disprove any of these views, but to intertwine them into one believable, logical and therefore probable view, not denying any scripture on the subject.   I will confine my explanation to the three viewpoints mentioned above.

Now, please read and discover for yourself that there in fact shall be *"three raptures"* of the Church: Pre-Tribulation; Mid-Tribulation; and Post-Tribulation.   Be comforted knowing if you or your loved ones miss the first rapture, you will have two other opportunities to meet the Lord in the air!

CHAPTER ONE

CONCEPT OF THE RAPTURE
(CATCHING AWAY)

The Holy Scriptures refer to the Bible in Christianity, the Tanakh and B'rit Chadashah in Judaism. Christians know the Lord as Jesus Christ, while Messianic Jews know Him as Yeshua (Savior) HaMashiach (The Anointed One) and traditional religious Jews know Him as Adonai/Hashem/HaMashiach. Scripture tells us in the *"Last Days"* the Lord will appear and rule the earth (Zechariah 14:9; Revelation 12:5; 19:15). For purposes of clarification, let me state Jesus for Christians and Yeshua for Messianic Jews are the same and I only separate them here because of the common usage in the language of each, Christianity and Judaism. I will utilize both, together, as we go forward separated by a forward slash.

From this point on, I will refer to the Holy Scriptures as the Bible because it contains both the Old Testament (Covenant) and New Testament. The Bible tells us in the book of Daniel, chapter 12 and the book of Matthew, chapter 24, there will be a time of trouble (tribulation) which the world has never experienced. In Revelation 3:10, we are told those who belong to the Lord will be protected from this time of Tribulation. This then becomes the core of this subject: how and when God will protect the Children of God. 1 Thessalonians 4:16, 17 tells us "the dead in Christ" and those who are alive in Christ *shall rise, "be caught up,"* and *"meet the Lord in the air."* This event commonly known as *The Rapture,* embodies three primary views as to when this *rapture* shall occur in reference to the end-time period of Tribulation: Pre-Tribulation, Mid-Tribulation or Post-Tribulation.

The Controversy Regarding the Rapture

This exegesis of the subject of the Lord Jesus Christ/Yeshua HaMashiach taking His body, the church, out of this world before, during and after the seven-year Tribulation Period, spoken of in the book of Daniel, chapters 9 and 12, is a result of:

1) revelation from the Holy Spirit

2) reading the Bible through several times

3) gaining an understanding of the story of the Bible

4) untangling the prophetic conclusion of the Bible

The Rapture (or catching away) is my rendering of a term used in the Bible which refers to an event which has caused considerable controversy in the Body of Christ/HaMashiach.

The passage in the Bible my term rapture refers to is:

Then we who are alive and remain shall be **caught up** together with them in the clouds to meet the Lord in the air. 1 Thessalonians 4:17a Emphasis added.

The term *caught up* is used in the context the Lord will take us up to meet Him in the air. Therefore, wherever the word rapture is used the reader is to understand it represents the catching away.

There are three basic passages of scripture upon which many positions regarding the title, *The Tri-Tribulation Rapture of The Church* are based. Because of this, much confusion has been caused regarding the subject. In order to explain the confusion caused by the different views of the Rapture, it is necessary to understand **the primary problem is it has to occur at only <u>one</u> of three points in time**. Each point in time is in reference to a seven-year period known as the Tribulation/Great Tribulation Period as spoken of in the books of Daniel, Matthew and 1 Thessalonians. The website NTEB (Now The End Begins), which includes a mention of a fourth viewpoint, the *"No Tribulation viewpoint,"* has this to say about these viewpoints:

> Anyone who has ever taken basic courses in Logic and Probability Outcomes will note that only one of these positions can be correct, as all four of them differ from each other in profound ways. (NTEB Pt. 1)

The basis of the various doctrines for the Rapture begins in Daniel 9:27, in which God tells Daniel there will come a time when a prince shall come and confirm (sign) a seven-year covenant (treaty). There is a second passage that has to do with our Lord Jesus Christ/Yeshua HaMashiach in Matthew 24:21, which states there will come a time of great tribulation the world has never experienced. Coupled with these two is a third passage by the Apostle Paul that states the Saints/Believers will be *"caught up"* (1 Thessalonians 4:17). From these three passages, the various viewpoints, along with supporting scriptures form the basis for their theories. The Rapture must, depending on your position, occur at a point either Pre-, Mid-, or Post-Tribulation in reference to the Great Tribulation Period. Those that agree with the Pre-Tribulation argument believe the Rapture must occur at or before the first stroke of signing the seven-year agreement by the anti-Christ/HaMashiach person, the prince of Daniel 9:26. The Mid-Tribulation belief is the Rapture will occur at the end of the first 3½-year point of this Tribulation/Great Tribulation Period. Then we have the Post-Tribulation Rapture conviction, which calls for the Rapture to occur near, at or even after the end of the Great Tribulation Period. In the voluminous amount of literature written on the subject of the Rapture, much or perhaps the majority is spent disproving opposing theories or viewpoints.

What these three primary views have caused in the Body of Christ is a division along these lines of when the Rapture will occur. Consequently, there has developed a very strong contention over which of these three versions is the correct one. Mind you, each of these versions come with the scriptural basis for why the Rapture should occur according to their belief, and rightly so.

If we really have God in Jesus Christ/Yeshua HaMashiach revealed in our hearts, then we know God is not the author of confusion (1 Corinthians 14:33). Therefore, because there are such unyielding supporters and much scriptural basis for each of the positions for the Rapture, there is appropriately a biblical justification for each. With this being the case, the three main views can come together and be joined as one in Christ, having clarity and purpose. This will allow the Body of Christ to be properly united in Him, Jesus Christ/Yeshua HaMashiach, the Name which is above every name, our Lord, our Savior, and our God. When achieved, scriptures that have caused controversy will be in their proper place to give clarity and cohesiveness to *The Tri-Tribulation Rapture of The Church.*

I think here is the proper place to further explain my use of the term *rapture and/or catching away.* I use the term *rapture* because it is the most well-known term used by both Christians and non-Christians. I use *catching away* for those who find the word rapture objectionable because it is not a word that can be transliterated (translated) from the Bible texts. In some places, I have **joined the two terms together in order to silence the argument as to which is the correct term**. In addition, the reader needs to understand I use both the English name for the Son of God, **Jesus**, and the Hebrew name, **Yeshua**. The correct name for a person is the name given in the language at birth. However, in different languages, an equivalent name is often given. This name then becomes common usage, as is the case for Jesus/Yeshua, English/Hebrew. **Therefore, I make use of both names combined with a slash**. I do the same for **Christ/HaMashiach**, which is English/Hebrew for the Anointed One/Messiah.

The term *caught up* is used universally in most versions of the Bible and not confined to the NKJV. It is used in the KJV, Amplified, NLV and even in the CJB to name a few. However, the term rapture came into the English language in the 14th century from the Middle English verb *ripen,* through the Latin noun *raptus,* and from the verb *rapere,* meaning to carry off which has a similar meaning. I use the term *catching away* rather than *caught up* to mean **from the viewpoint of the event happening in the present** and not in the future because whenever it happens, it will be in the present. I point this out to minimize the confusion and not add to it.

Finally, I will use and capitalize the word *Believer* rather than use the word *saint* to refer to those who have received Jesus Christ/Yeshua HaMashiach as Lord, Savior, and God so as not to confuse anyone to whether there is any connotation of idolatry (referring to the Catholics use of Saint). Where saint is used, I will capitalize and couple it with Believer. Also, I will use a lower case *non* that is hyphenated with a capitalized *Believer* (non-Believer) to indicate one who is not in the Kingdom of God.

Before beginning, let us address the question of which biblical text to use. The Rapture is a concept from the Bible. Because we are addressing a biblical subject, if one cannot accept the Bible as the authoritative reference on the subject, then he or she will not be able to discern or receive the concept of the Rapture fully, if at all. The premise in beginning is the Bible, whether Old or New Testament, is true. The question becomes which version is the correct or most correct and true. It is my opinion all of the recognized and accepted translations are true. It is also true each version may differ in some specific meaning contextually, as to how it is written and what is its meaning. This may be true in the general context of what God is saying and yet its impartation be in complete agreement in every version. After all, God has spoken to all peoples in all dispensations and eras to bring order, peace, salvation, purpose, and direction into their lives. I believe the Bible answers all questions in all facets, areas, situations, and conditions in everyone's life. The Bible says in Revelation 22:17, "'Come!' And let him who thirsts come. Whoever desires let him take the water of life freely." This statement is translated slightly different in some translations, but the meaning is the same in all: regardless of who you are, male or female, black or white, Jew or Gentile, drug addict or drug free, intelligent or imbecile; all may come and find their answers to life's problems and questions. These answers are found in our Lord, Savior, and God, Jesus Christ/Yeshua HaMashiach, the Word of God (John 1:1-18). **In lieu of the above, the primary text used here will be the New King James Version (NKJV), unless otherwise noted**. You may find an excellent, more thorough explanation of Bible translations and versions in the introduction of the Complete Jewish Bible by David H. Stern (Stern xiv).

I will present the Rapture in a clear, concise and understandable manner so anyone, whether novice or theologian, can grasp it. Further, after having read this presentation, the reader will come away with the idea that **until the Lord returns, there are more than one opportunity of being raptured into the presence of the Lord. It will also be comforting to know all is not lost if he or she should miss the first or second rapture event.**

My hope is after having read this presentation of the subject matter, the reader will also be comforted by the knowledge he or she has gained. Perhaps then the reader will have hope, joy, and peace in his or her personal selection of which view he or she chooses to embrace. In addition, I make note of the terms **hope** and **comfort** to reassure the reader the Rapture **is not a subject to frighten or be a source of worry, but to be one of hope, comfort and security for those who have a true relationship with Jesus Christ/Yeshua HaMashiach.** Paul says to the Thessalonians in 1Thessalonians 4:13, "… lest you sorrow as others who have no hope," meaning those who have not made Jesus Christ/Yeshua HaMashiach their Lord and Savior have no hope of salvation. This is of course until they do repent and receive Jesus/Yeshua as their Lord, Savior, and God. We who have confessed Jesus Christ/Yeshua HaMashiach as Lord and Savior in our heart not only have hope but are assured of salvation, which is eternal life and in that is comfort and security.

Furthermore, I have in some places attempted to make the understanding of this context more effective by inserting a word in parentheses, which is more generally understood than the word used in the context of the sentence.

In order to prepare for the presentation of the revelation I believe the Lord has given me, I will give an overview of the current view or theory of each: The Pre-Tribulation, Mid-Tribulation and Post-Tribulation Rapture events. Be mindful each of these views has proponents; those who believe their view is the correct one and have gone to great lengths to prove their view is the only correct view (Kinsella). The major problem in all of the views is each one has to put aside scripture that supports the Rapture but does not fit their viewpoint. Secondary to this is the disagreement as to which view a particular scripture is pointing. As we all know, no matter how great our revelation is, we cannot say it is the final revelation on a matter. Having said that, **the reader can enjoy this presentation and understand there may be greater and more in-depth revelation to come regarding the Rapture.**

Before addressing the subject of the Rapture, there are more views than those stated above regarding the Rapture. There is the **preterist** view which says the rapture has already occurred. In fact, they say all events pertaining to Jesus/Yeshua's Second Advent were essentially fulfilled by the year 70 A.D. and because of that, we are now living in the Post-Tribulation Period and are in the everlasting Kingdom of God (Simmons). According to Richard Anthony:

> The "catching-up" (1 Thess. 4:17) or "gathering" (Matt. 24:31) was accomplished when the faithful remnant of Jewish believers with the in-grafted Gentiles were transformed (and transferred) into Christ's new spiritual Israel. This was accomplished at the same time the old fleshly-based Israel was dissolved at A.D. 70.

After giving an extensive account of his preterist view Todd Dennis reports, "Therefore, there is no future seven-year tribulation period." Preterists say and believe Jesus/Yeshua predicted and fulfilled His second coming during the lifetime of His apostles (Simmons). Then there is the **amillennial** view of the End Time. This view as suggested by Anthony Hoekema in his article on amillennialism, is there is only a continual millennial reign of Jesus/Yeshua from His resurrection from the dead. Therefore, there is only a Church Age in which the church is to develop and bring to fruition the final state of the Kingdom of God, Luke 17:20, 21 (Hoekema 2). They do not believe the rapture is a separate event or events from the Second Advent of Jesus/Yeshua. They say what the other viewpoints believe, regarding the rapture, is merely the Saints/Believers going up into the clouds to meet Jesus/Yeshua and returning to earth with Him at the Advent of Christ/HaMashiach (Hoekema 5). Beyond these there are many other interpretations regarding the *Last Days, End of Days, or Time of the End*, depending on the passage, version of the Bible, or viewpoint you are reading, which may or may not include a rapture event. There are also those who believe the more difficult concepts in the Bible are more symbolic than anything and not taken as literal events. However, fundamentally speaking regarding the rapture, there are three principle views which I mentioned in the opening paragraph: The Pre-, Mid-, and Post-Tribulation views. Therefore, for our purposes, these three fundamental views are the ones to which we will be primarily confined.

In order to get the most out of what the reader shall read, one must be born again by receiving Jesus Christ/Yeshua HaMashiach as Lord, Savior, and God. To become born again, just ask Jesus to become Lord, Savior, and God of your life and He will do so; trust me. Then you will receive greater understanding as to what is being presented. A prayer for salvation is given on the following page to assist you in greater insight on this subject, but even greater in magnitude, you will receive everlasting life.

To receive **LIFE FOR ALL ETERNITY**; what can be greater than that?

SALVATION PRAYER

To receive your salvation and become born again scripture says:

...that if you confess with your mouth the Lord Jesus and believe in your heart that God has raised Him from the dead, you will be saved. For with the heart one believes unto righteousness, and with the mouth confession is made unto salvation. Romans 10:9, 10

The fact the scripture says you should "confess with your mouth," indicates the prayer should be said aloud. A prayer that accomplishes this, coupled with believing in your heart, can be read aloud as follows:

Dear heavenly Father, I come to You now, just as I am. You know everything about my life; forgive me my sins, Lord. I repent of all my sins. Now according to Your word in Romans chapter 10:9, 10, I believe Jesus Christ is the Son of God and He died for my sins. On the third day, He was raised from the dead and He is alive right now. Lord Jesus, I ask You to come into my heart, live Your life in and through me, from this day forward I belong to You.

Now to receive the fullness of what God has for you, ask Him to fill you with His Holy Spirit by saying:

Lord, I pray for and thank You right now, for filling me with Your Holy Spirit with the evidence of speaking in my heavenly language. I declare right now I am healed, I am whole, I am redeemed and I praise You for it in Jesus' name, Amen.

NOW SAY, "I AM A BORN-AGAIN BELIEVER!"

Welcome into the Kingdom of God!

CHAPTER TWO

DEFINING THE RAPTURE AND THE GREAT TRIBULATION

Let us lay the groundwork for discussing the Rapture views. The different views agree the Rapture will occur in reference to **the 70th week** in the book of Daniel. It is generally accepted the passage from Daniel 9:24-27 is speaking of 70 weeks and each day of each week represents one year. To understand the concept of *weeks of years,* I refer you to the explanation of weeks of years in the book of Leviticus:

> And you shall count seven sabbaths of years
> for yourself, seven times seven years; and
> the time of the seven sabbaths of years shall
> be to you forty-nine years. Leviticus 25:8

Therefore, it speaks of seven years for each week (sabbath) times 70 weeks, (7x70=490). The passage in Daniel also speaks of seven plus 62 weeks or 69 weeks of years (7+62x7) equals 483 years until Messiah the Prince, which refers to the coming of Jesus Christ/Yeshua HaMashiach and His death, burial and resurrection. This leaves the final seven years of the prophecy yet to be fulfilled. **The final seven years will be the Tribulation/Great Tribulation Period.** Most Bible scholars say this final seven-year period has been set aside for a period of time which will be, or is determined by God the Father, for the purpose of allowing Gentiles (non-Believers) from all nations of the world to be saved (Romans chapters 9-11). Therefore, it is believed this will end before or at the time of the Great Tribulation Period. In other words, God's greater emphasis, from the resurrection of Jesus Christ/Yeshua HaMashiach until the start of the 70th week of Daniel 9:24, is to have non-Jewish people receive salvation (Romans 11:25). This is not to say Jews are not to be saved. Paul the apostle suggests to the Romans:

> You will say then, "Branches were broken off that I might be grafted in." Well said. Because of unbelief they were broken off, and you stand by faith. Do not be haughty, but fear. For if God did not spare the natural branches. He may not spare you either. Therefore, consider the goodness and severity of God: on those who fell, severity; but toward you, goodness, if you continue in His goodness. Otherwise you also will be cut off. And they also, if they do not continue in unbelief will be grafted in, for God is able to graft them in again. Romans 11:19-23

Jesus Christ/Yeshua HaMashiach refers to the book of Daniel and the Great Tribulation in the book of Matthew:

Therefore, when you see the 'abomination of desolation,' spoken of by Daniel the prophet standing in the holy place (whoever reads, let him understand), then let those who are in Judea flee to the mountains. Let him who is on the housetop not go down to take anything out of his house. And let him who is in the field not go back to get his clothes. But woe to those who are pregnant and to those who are nursing babies in those days! And pray that your flight may not be in winter or on the Sabbath. For then there will be great tribulation, such as has not been since the beginning of the world until this time, no, nor ever shall be. And unless those days were shortened, no flesh would be saved; but for the elect's sake those days will be shortened. Matthew 24:15-22

This refers to Daniel chapter 9:

Then he shall confirm a covenant with many for one week; but in the middle of the week He shall bring an end to sacrifice and offering. And on the wing of abominations shall be one who makes desolate, even until the consummation, which is determined, is poured out on the desolate. Daniel 9:27

Notice Jesus/Yeshua said: "abomination of desolation" and both words are in Daniel 9:27. Furthermore, the verse says one week. The week is a week of years, seven years. The week will begin by a covenant (treaty) being made for seven years. It further says the prince who is to come, as referred to in verse 26, is the signer of the treaty (the one who confirms) and in the "middle of the week," he will be the one who makes desolate. **The final thing to note is Jesus/Yeshua is speaking of a future event, which tells us any reference to any abomination that occurs in the Old Testament is not that of Daniel 9:27.** In addition, He tells us **this will be the greatest time of tribulation the world has ever known to that point (Matthew 24:21).**

Therefore, we have a **seven-year period launched by the signing of a treaty** during which a terrible change or changes occur in the middle of the week. Because Daniel 9:27 makes reference to the middle of the week, it defines three phases to this seven-year period. Therefore, we can say we have a pre-period phase, which is that time leading up to and including any time before the signing of the treaty. There is also a mid-period phase, which would be any time closer to the mid-point (3½ years) than to either the beginning or end of the seven-year period. Finally, there is a post-period phase, which would be near, at or after the end of the tribulation period. **Hence, we have Pre-, Mid-, and Post-Tribulation period phases or points to this seven-year tribulation period Jesus Christ/Yeshua HaMashiach speaks of.** In addition, the Lord makes mention unless the days are shortened, no flesh shall be saved. Now, what does this statement mean? This is answered in the following scripture:

> Thus says the Lord: "As the new wine is found in the cluster, and one says, 'Do not

destroy it, for a blessing is in it.' So will I do for My servants' sake, that I may not destroy them all. Isaiah 65:8

Why is it important to know about the Rapture?

It is important to know and understand the rapture because it or they will occur during a very specific time in our future. That time is for all intents and purposes not too distant in our future. If according to the Bible, in several books of the Old Testament/Tanakh and the New Testament, Jesus Christ/Yeshua HaMashiach will take His Body, the Church, out of this world it is of paramount importance to know what the requirement is to be sure you will be in the rapture(s). In a few words, the requirement to participate in the rapture is to receive Jesus Christ/Yeshua HaMashiach as your Lord, Savior, and God. In other words, to be saved.

The Apostle Paul was sent, by the Lord Jesus Christ/Yeshua HaMashiach, to the Gentiles to give them the opportunity to receive salvation. Though the rapture did not occur during his lifetime he considered it extremely important for the Believers to understand the procedure of the rapture event. To the Believers in the city of Thessalonica, who were confused about who was going in the rapture he offered this explanation,

But I do not want you to be ignorant, brethren, concerning those who have fallen asleep, **lest you sorrow as others who have no hope.** For if we believe that Jesus died and rose again, even so God will bring with

Him those who sleep [have died] in Jesus. For this we say to you by the word of the Lord, that **we who are alive and remain until the coming of the Lord** will by no means precede those who are asleep [have died]. For the Lord Himself will descend from heaven with a shout, with the voice of an archangel, and with the trumpet of God. And the dead in Christ will rise first. **Then we who are alive and remain shall be caught up together [raptured] with them in the clouds to meet the Lord in the air.** And thus we shall always be with the Lord. 1Thessalonians 4:13-17. Emphasis added.

Being this is a very definite event which Paul speaks of, it is fitting for us to be as knowledgeable as we can about when it should occur. Also, it is understood he is **speaking very definitely** to those who are **in Christ**. When he speaks of those who are *dead in Christ,* meaning Believers who have died, then by extension, the same applies to Believers who are *alive and remain*. Again, Paul says we, those who are watchful in Christ, shall not participate in the **Great Tribulation**:

Therefore let us not sleep, as others do, but let us watch and be sober. For those who sleep, sleep at night, and those who get drunk are drunk at night. But let us who are of the day be sober, putting on the breastplate of faith and love, and as a helmet the hope of salvation. **For God did not appoint us to wrath,** but to obtain salvation through our Lord Jesus Christ, who died for us, that whether we wake [are alive] or sleep [die], we should live together with Him. Therefore comfort each other and edify one another, just as you also are doing. 1Thessalonians 5:2-11. Emphasis added.

There are four points in this passage Paul makes which I believe make it clear as to why it is important for us to know about the Great Tribulation Period, the Rapture and the relationship between the two. Paul says,

• "Let us watch and be sober." We should ever be looking for the coming of the Lord; not in a frenzy, but in a mature and calm attitude of expectation.

• "…, putting on the breastplate of faith and love, and as a helmet the hope of salvation." We are to exercise faith, love, and hope until He comes, trying to win as many souls as we can until we are raptured.

• "God did not appoint us to wrath, but to obtain salvation through our Lord Jesus Christ." God does not intend to allow those in Christ to go through the wrath of the Tribulation Period, but to begin their eternal life with Him. Also, to "obtain salvation" in this context is to be saved from danger as in the exodus of the Israelites from Egypt, going through the Red Sea. Moses raised his staff and spoke, "do not be afraid, stand still, and see the salvation of the Lord, which He will accomplish for you today" (Exodus 14:13). This, the Lord did the very day He said He would deliver them out of danger from Pharaoh.

• "Comfort each other and edify one another," meaning when we have received Jesus/Yeshua as Lord, we can then reassure one another and teach one another to look for His coming and be assured when He comes we will be with Him forevermore.

Finally, Jesus/Yeshua said to His disciples in Matthew 24:22, if the days before His coming were not "shortened, **no** flesh would be saved; but for the elect's sake those days will be shortened." Emphasis added. This I believe is a related scripture to Revelation 14:12-16, which suggests the Lord will catch-up His Believers/Saints before God's final wrath of Revelation 17. After Revelation 14:16, there is no more reference to salvation or to Believers until Revelation 19:7; the Marriage Supper of the Lamb and the armies of heaven that return with the Lord to reign on the earth.

For these reasons, it is very important for Believers to know and understand the Rapture. We can be comforted in knowing we *know* Christ (1 John 2:3), and we are His "special treasure in earthen vessels" (2 Corinthians 4:7). We are special enough not to have to go through *the Great Tribulation.* In addition, knowing this will put urgency in telling those we love and those we know to receive the Lord as Savior as the day approaches. Then they too can be comforted, knowing they do not have to endure the Great Tribulation Period as the Lord mentioned in Matthew 24:21.

Only God the Father knows when the events of the *last days* will occur, (Acts 1:7), therefore, no calculations can pinpoint any event, in the future. We must recognize our God determines times and seasons according to His own reckoning, not ours (Matthew 24:36). However, once the Tribulation Period begins, we know it will last seven years because of the 70-year prophecy in Jeremiah 25:11, which has to be completed according to Daniel 9:24-27.

Why is the Great Tribulation Necessary?

Now, some explanation of why the Great Tribulation is necessary. In other words, explain why God would pour out His wrath upon the earth? God created mankind in order to have fellowship with a being that has the choice to love Him or not. The choice not to love Him carries the consequence of being separated from God. God's original intent was all would be able to be in His presence, to love and enjoy fellowship with Him, for all eternity.

> The Lord is not slack concerning His promise, as some count slackness, but is longsuffering toward us, not willing that any should perish, but that all should come to repentance. 2 Peter 3:9

Through choice, man broke fellowship with God. This came through the disobedience of Adam in the Garden of Eden (Genesis 3:6). God put man out of the garden because He cannot fellowship with evil. Therefore, man had to dwell outside of the garden and gradually became utterly wicked. God judged the world that existed then by bringing a flood (2 Peter 3:5-6). However, He saved eight people from His wrath: Noah and his family (Genesis 6), which is a type and shadow of the rapture.

After the flood, mankind began to repopulate the earth. Again, and almost immediately, the people began to be corrupted by sin (Genesis 9:20). However, rather than destroy all again, God chose to redeem them by bringing forth a savior (Galatians 3:16). This redeemer had to be perfect because only a perfect and holy person could redeem mankind from all sin (Galatians 4:3-7). This person would have to sacrifice himself as a ransom for all and for all time (Hebrews 10:12-14). Therefore, God chose Abraham, the eleventh generation from Noah, and through his progeny, dating from the flood over the course of approximately 2000 years, produced the Savior, Jesus the Christ/Yeshua HaMashiach.

> Therefore, as through one man's offense judgment came to all men, resulting in condemnation, even so through one Man's righteous act the free gift came to all men, resulting in justification of life. For as by one man's disobedience many were made sinners, so also by one Man's obedience many will be made righteous. Romans 5:18, 19

Now, this had to be done in order that man could be allowed into the presence of God, for He cannot dwell in the presence of evil (Hebrews 3:7-19).

Pastor Bill Winston has summed up or pictured the necessity for a redeemer this way (to paraphrase him):

> Because of Adam's sin in the Garden of Eden, all are born in sin because all of mankind began or came from Adam and Eve. Therefore, sin is imputed, ascribed, or accredited to all who have been born since then. So, in a sense, all souls are or have been pawned into the pawn shop of Satan. In order for a soul to be redeemed from the pawn shop, a ticket of redemption must be presented by a redeemer. Our souls are redeemed by our one and only Redeemer, Jesus Christ/Yeshua HaMashiach. The ticket for our redemption was the shedding of innocent blood, the death, burial and resurrection of Jesus Christ/Yeshua HaMashiach.

The redeeming of our soul is by receiving and believing He died for our sin, was buried, and He Himself, God the Father and the Holy Spirit raised Him from the dead (John 10:17; Romans 8:11; 10:9, 10).

This is because God is full of grace and gives grace, mercy, love, and forgiveness to all those that call upon the name of the Lord Jesus Christ/Yeshua HaMashiach.

After the death, burial, and resurrection of Jesus Christ/Yeshua HaMashiach, the Church Age officially began and has continued for approximately 2000 years. Now at His ascension, Acts 1:9-11, two men in white apparel said to those standing by:

Men of Galilee, why do you stand gazing up into heaven? This same Jesus, who was taken up from you into heaven, will so come in like manner as you saw Him go into heaven.

It is generally understood the two men standing nearby were angels. The importance of the statement is **the Lord will return**. In Matthew 25:31, Jesus speaks of the Son of Man coming in His glory and judging the nations, separating the sheep from the goats, which is separating the righteous from the wicked. Now, this scripture can be construed to mean Jesus will not separate the righteous from the wicked until the last judgment, at the White Throne mentioned in Revelation 20:11. However, it more properly pertains to an all-encompassing time in which Jesus separates the righteous from the wicked which includes the Rapture and the Great White Throne Judgment. What we must keep in mind is **God is not the author of confusion and He is not a man that He would or even could lie** (Numbers 23:19). Therefore, when all things are taken into account, all of it must make perfect sense.

Our foundational scripture, Hebrews 13:8, "Jesus Christ is the same yesterday, today and forever" gives us the basis of the *why* for God's wrath. God judged the world in Noah's day (Genesis 6:13, 14). God judged Sodom and Gomorrah for their iniquity (Genesis 19:12, 13). God judged Egypt and Canaan in delivering Israel into the Promised Land because of the iniquity of the peoples (ten nations) in the land (Genesis 15:19-21;

Exodus 14). Jesus Christ/Yeshua HaMashiach said His coming would be compared with the days of Noah. He also spoke of the coming of the Son of Man (Matthew 24:29-31, 36-44). All of the above will be in fulfillment of Isaiah 9:6, 7:

> For unto us a Child is born, Unto us a Son is given; And the government will be upon His shoulder. And His name will be called Wonderful, Counselor, Mighty God, Everlasting Father, Prince of Peace. **Of the increase of His government and peace there will be no end**, upon the throne of David and over His kingdom, to order it with judgment and **justice from that time forward, even forever.** The zeal of the Lord of host will perform this. Emphasis added.

Therefore, we see God has a limit to iniquity, violence and lawlessness; He *will* judge His creation. However, He has prepared a place for those who *will* choose Him (John 14:1-3). However, He must judge the earth and all people who do not choose Him.

For those who choose to give their hearts to Him, the Apostle Paul writes:

> For God did not appoint us to wrath, but to obtain salvation through our Lord Jesus Christ, who died for us, that whether we wake or sleep, we should live together with Him. 1Thessalonians 5:9, 10

This he said after his explanation of the rapture, we are not appointed by God to experience **wrath** but have **salvation** through Jesus/Yeshua. **Wrath,** meaning the *Day of the Lord* is referred to in verse 2 of the chapter. **Salvation,** meaning **saved or delivered** from the wrath, is **not the saving of our soul** for he was speaking to **Believers** whose souls are **already saved**. We can make an analogy to the Israelites being saved from facing the wrath of Pharaoh at the Red Sea when Moses said, "Stand still, and see the salvation of the Lord" (Exodus 14:13). The Complete Jewish Bible renders this as "Stop being so fearful! Remain steady, and you will see how Adonai is going to save you" (Stern 75). I point out to the reader the term salvation is used to indicate God, the Lord, will save us out of a wrathful crisis. In fact, the word, in Hebrew, for Salvation is actually the name of our Lord, Yeshua, which means salvation! **Just as He did in the Old Testament, He will also do in the New Testament**. Hebrews 13:8 says, "Jesus Christ is the same yesterday, today, and forever."

Therefore, we are assured to miss or not experience the wrath promised in *The Day of the Lord/The Great Tribulation,* which is necessary in order to cleanse the earth of all iniquity in order to bring about a new heaven and a new earth, free of evil for His people in eternity, Revelation 21:1.

Biblical Precedents for the Rapture

Since our subject is the Rapture, the question is, are we able to find any precedent in which there was a rapture by God or the Lord? Yes, I believe we can. The first precedent was set forth in the book of Genesis:

> So all the days of Enoch were three hundred
> and sixty-five years and Enoch walked with
> God; and he was not, for God took him.
> Genesis 5:23, 24

We know this is a rapture because Jared, who fathered Enoch, died and Methuselah, who was Enoch's son, died also. However, scripture says, "Enoch walked with God; and he was not, _**for God took him.**_" Emphasis added. The only explanation for this sudden change from all others in the lineage is there was a rapture. **For all others it stated they died.** This rapture occurred before the Flood, which destroyed all of mankind except for Noah's family of eight people.

The next precedent occurs in the book of 2 Kings:

> Then it happened, as they continued on and
> talked that suddenly a chariot of fire
> appeared with horses of fire, and separated
> the two of them; and Elijah went up by a
> whirlwind into heaven. 2 Kings 2: 11

In this passage, we not only have a catching away, but also a visible component to the catching away. Elisha witnessed the event, the rapture of Elijah, because he was seeking the God of Elijah diligently and being watchful in order to receive a double portion of the anointing that was on Elijah. As the passage continues, there were others who did not see the event because it was a supernatural event and events in the supernatural are seldom seen by every bystander. Therefore, the likelihood is, at the moment of its occurring, and **because it will take place in an instant, if you are not raptured you will not be aware it has even occurred.** In the time directly following the event, all who are not raptured will come to the glaring realization something earth-shattering has happened.

Next is the Apostle Paul's being caught up to the third heaven, in 2 Corinthians:

> I know a man in Christ who fourteen years ago – whether in the body I do not know, or whether out of the body I do not know, God knows – such a one was **caught up** to the third heaven. And I know such a man – whether in the body or out of the body I do not know, God knows – how he was **caught up** into Paradise and heard inexpressible words, which it is not lawful for a man to utter. 2 Corinthians 12:2-4 Emphasis added.

Apparently, Paul was caught up to the third heaven in an instant, as it would happen in a rapture, and was so awestruck it was difficult to express the experience. His experience, though awesome, is not so unheard of today. There are many testimonies of Believers and non-Believers being raptured or caught up to heaven. Every one of them convey they would have rather stayed in heaven but the Lord told them He was sending them back with a message for us. That message is to be saved and be ready to be raptured.

Finally, there is John in the book of Revelation:

> After these things I looked, and behold, a door standing open in heaven. And the first voice which I heard was like a trumpet speaking with me, saying, "Come up here, and I will show you things which must take place after this." Immediately I was in the Spirit and behold, a throne set in heaven, and One sat on the throne. Revelation 4:1, 2

Here we have the Apostle John, the last of the 12 apostles. John has been exiled to the island of Patmos in the Aegean Sea. He is receiving a revelation from Jesus Christ/Yeshua HaMashiach. He is told by Jesus/Yeshua in Revelation 1:19 "Write the things which you have seen, and the things which are, and the things which will take place after this." The things which will take place after this begins at chapter 4, verse one, in which John is raptured/caught up to heaven and into the Throne Room of God. John was summoned up to the Throne Room by a voice, which said, "Come up here, and I will show you things which must take place after this. Immediately I was in the Spirit," Revelation 4:1b, 2a. Then he wrote of the things he saw and heard.

What I have done here is demonstrate from the biblical text there are examples of living people in the Word of God who were raptured.

The foregoing is written to give those who have not done a great deal of studying or reading the Word of God a degree of understanding which will allow them to follow that which is written hereafter. We shall delve into each of the three major viewpoints for the rapture, after which I will present how all three viewpoints will come together into one all-inclusive viewpoint in chapter 7, *My Reconciliation of the Tri-Tribulation Rapture.*

As it says in the scripture:

And we know that all things work together for good to those who love God, to those who are the called according to His purpose. Romans 8:28

CHAPTER THREE

THE PRE-TRIBULATION RAPTURE VIEWPOINT

In all of the viewpoints we discuss, Pre-, Mid- and Post-Tribulation rapture, the question is not whether or not there is to be a rapture, but in which season and when shall it occur. I am presenting the basic scriptural basis for each viewpoint as there is a sound basis for each. All viewpoints regarding the rapture must deal with the following major points:

➤ What is the scriptural basis for the viewpoint?
➤ Who is the Church and who will be left behind?
➤ How long are the Tribulation and Great Tribulation periods?
➤ When does the wrath of God begin and how long does it last?
➤ When does the rapture occur according to this viewpoint?
➤ What do opposing viewpoints say regarding the validity of the viewpoint under discussion?

The above points will not apply equally to each of the theories discussed due to limitations of each theory.

Scriptural Basis for the Pre-Tribulation Rapture

Pre-tribulationists believe the rapture is the event which will signal the onset of the time that is spoken of in the book of Jeremiah 30:7, "as the time of Jacob's trouble;" in the book of Daniel 9:27 regarding the **treaty "with many for one week";** in Matthew 24:21 and in Daniel 12:1-4 "a time of trouble, such as never was since there was a nation." They say the pre-tribulation viewpoint follows a literal interpretation" of Scripture, Old and New Testament.

Basic scriptures for the Pre-Tribulation Rapture viewpoint:

- Believers will not experience the wrath of God (Romans 5:9; Ephesians 5:6; Colossians 3:6; 1 Thessalonians 1:10, 5:9; Revelation 3:10).
- The Second Advent (Second Coming) will be at the end of the Tribulation Period (Revelation 19:11-20).
- There has to be time to give rewards to the Believers before the Lord's Second Coming (1Corinthins 3:12 - 15).
- The rapture of the Church occurs at Revelation 4 with the rapture of Apostle John.
- Because there is no mention of the Church after Revelation Chapter 3 the Church has been raptured and is in heaven.

Pre-tribulationists believe the rapture is imminent and no prophecy needs fulfilling before it can occur. In the Pre-Tribulation Rapture viewpoint, the central most scripture is:

> ...and to wait for His Son from heaven, whom He raised from the dead, even Jesus who delivers us from the wrath to come. 1 Thessalonians 1:10

The key point in the above quote for the Pre-tribulationist is, Paul tells the Thessalonians Jesus will deliver them "from the wrath to come." Therefore, the Church, the body of Jesus Christ/Yeshua HaMashiach, will avoid experiencing the wrath, which is to come upon the whole earth. They believe because Paul was speaking to Believers in Christ/HaMashiach, both Jews and Gentiles, what he spoke was only for the Church.

Pre-tribulationists say the fact Noah being saved from the flood in the ark and Lot taken out of Sodom and Gomorrah are types of rapture in the Old Testament/Covenant and confirms God will save His people at the time of the Tribulation Period. Finally, Pre-tribulationists say all the scriptures referring to the Tribulation Period make no mention of the Church. Therefore, the Church is not present in the Tribulation Period.

Who is the Church and who will be left behind?

We should define who the Church is, according to the Pre-tribulationist's viewpoint, because it has a material effect on how the events of the Tribulation Period unfold in relation to when the rapture occurs.

The Church is comprised of all born-again Christians. That is to say all who have confessed the Lord Jesus as their Lord and Savior and have believed in their hearts that God raised Him from the dead.

...that if you confess with your mouth the Lord Jesus and believe in your **heart** that God has raised Him from the dead, you will be saved. For with the heart one believes unto righteousness, and with the mouth confession is made unto salvation. Romans 10:9, 10 Emphasis added.

This is true for all whether they were Jews or Gentiles; they are now Believers in Jesus Christ/Yeshua HaMashiach and made righteous by the blood of Jesus Christ, Yeshua/HaMashiach.

For He made Him who knew no sin to be sin for us, that we might become the righteousness of God in Him. II Corinthians 5:21

The Pre-Tribulationists believe all of these will be taken at the Rapture.

Anyone who receives Christ/HaMashiach as their Lord and Savior after the Rapture will have to go through the entire Tribulation Period. By and large the Pre-Tribulationists believe that those who will be saved during the Tribulation Period will be Jews and the Tribulation Period will serve as a time of purification. The Church does not need purification and is therefore raptured prior to the Tribulation Period while all saved during the period will have to go through it and at the Second Coming of

Jesus/Christ, Yeshua/HaMashiach go into the Millennium and be subjects to be ruled during it.

How long are the Tribulation and Great Tribulation Periods?

The pre-tribulation belief based on the 70th week of years, according to Daniel 9:27, the **Tribulation and Great Tribulation Period will be seven years. The week will be divided into two 3½-year periods.**

To sum up the Pre-Tribulation view of the length of the Tribulation Period and the Great Tribulation Period. The Tribulation Period is the first 3 ½ years while the Great Tribulation is the second 3 ½ years but there are those who believe the entire seven-year period is the Great Tribulation Period. The Pre-Tribulationists believe their view is the only view that accurately interprets the Scriptures regarding the Tribulation Period and The Rapture. Because, they say, their view is based on a literal interpretation of the Scriptures.

When does the wrath of God begin and how long does it last?

From the Pre-tribulationists viewpoint, because the Church is not appointed to wrath (1 Thessalonians 1:10, 5:9), it is key to establish when the wrath of God begins because at that point the Church will not be here.

To proceed, if we are not appointed to wrath, then it is certain the rapture will precede any wrath of the Lamb and/or wrath of God poured out on the earth during the

Tribulation/Great Tribulation Period. Therefore, Pre-Tribulationists consider the opening of the sixth seal to be the beginning of the Wrath of God (the Lamb). By definition, the Pre-Tribulation Rapture could not occur during or after the Tribulation Period is over! This could not be, because the wrath of God is an integral (essential) part of the Tribulation/Great Tribulation Period. Therefore, Pre-tribulationists consider the entire seven-year period to be the wrath of God and say the Church will not be present to experience God's wrath.

When does the Rapture occur according to this viewpoint?

The book of Revelation tells us:

I looked when He opened the sixth seal, and behold there was a great earthquake; ... For the great day of His wrath has come, and who is able to stand? Revelation 6:12, 17

This passage of scripture is from the sixth seal of the scroll of God, which is opened by the Lamb of God, Jesus/Yeshua. What follows from this seal, when opened, is the people of the earth, both small and great, are so ravished by an earthquake and other physical disasters that they cry out and claim the great day of the wrath of God has come. Therefore, a Pre-Tribulation Rapture would have to happen before this point, according to Revelation 6:12.

Most Pre-tribulationists say after Revelation 4:1, the Church is not mentioned any longer therefore this represents the Rapture. John, who received the revelation from Jesus Christ/Yeshua HaMashiach, was raptured up to the throne room of God. The Pre-tribulationists point out this catching up of John into heaven precedes the events of the Tribulation and/or Great Tribulation Period; it is a foreshadowing of, and therefore confirms the rapture of the church will occur before the Great Tribulation.

Bill Burns, on his CD regarding his *A STUDY IN REVELATION: Seven Seals,* makes an interesting point in saying the Pre-Tribulation Rapture event occurs before the Tribulation Period. He says this is because the earthquake in Revelation 6:14 announces the rapture event. He believes the receding sky is God's way of allowing the raptured Saints/Believers an entrance into heaven. He explains the receding, like a scroll, is the rolling back of the sky making a doorway into heaven like the door which John sees in Revelation 4:1 (Burns 39:22-39:58).

The fact Holy Spirit will be removed will be confirmation the Church has been raptured.

> For the mystery of lawlessness is already at work; only He who now restrains will do so until He is taken out of the way. II Thessalonians 2:7

Pre-Tribulationists say that Paul here is saying that during the Tribulation Period the Holy Spirit will be completely taken out and that will be proof positive the rapture has occurred.

They say the description in Revelation chapter 5 of the one hundred million plus viewers before the throne of God include the Pre-Tribulation saints, as well as the angels, elders, living creatures and Believers/Saints since the Garden of Eden. If so, then it is evident the rapture occurs before the entire Tribulation Period, which begins with the wrath of God at Revelation 6:12 and the opening of the sixth seal.

What do opposing viewpoints have to say regarding the Pre-Tribulation Rapture?

The Mid-Tribulationists say their view requires less alteration to fit a pre-millennial interpretation of the Tribulation Period. They say Believers will have to endure *some* of the tribulation of the Tribulation Period. In addition, Mid-Tribulationists point to the Bible more accurately and consistently divides the period into two major periods. Each one is 3½ years and basically makes consistent references to it in Daniel, chapters 7:25; 9:24-27; 12:7-12 and Revelation 11:2-3; 12:6; 12:14; 13:5. This is all without violating end-time discourses in Matthew, Mark and Luke.

Post-Tribulationists position the wrath of God at the very end of the Tribulation Period. The position the Church is no longer present after the rapture event which occurs before the Tribulation Period is untenable. Pre-tribulation requires two different plans for salvation. Besides, if Christ's/HaMashiach's death is a once for all covenant, then the Pre-Tribulation argument, which states the Believers/Saints of the Tribulation Period are not part of the Church cannot be. There are Believers/Saints in the Tribulation Period, therefore, there can be no Pre-Tribulation Rapture

CHAPTER FOUR

THE MID-TRIBULATION RAPTURE VIEWPOINT

Mid-tribulationists have several variations on the theory of the Mid-Tribulation Rapture. The theory the Mid-Tribulation Rapture will occur at the mid-point of Daniel's 70th week began in 1941 by Norman B. Harrison in his book, *The End: Rethinking the Revelation* (Vaterhaus). The most prevalent view is the rapture will occur at the exact middle of the Tribulation Period. It is believed by them the Antichrist will be revealed at that point in time and the Wrath of God will begin to be poured out at that time.

Like the Pre-Tribulationists they believe the rapture will happen before the Second Coming of the Lord Jesus Christ/Yeshua HaMashiach.

The Scriptural Basis for Mid-Tribulation Rapture

The Mid-tribulationists believe the Tribulation Period is divided into two halves. They believe the Mid-Tribulation Rapture fulfills scripture more completely than either of the other two positions because the rapture will occur exactly at the middle of the Tribulation Period, leaving two halves of three and one-half years each.

Daniel 7:25, 9:27; 12:7 along with Revelation 11:2, 3; 12:6, 14; 13:5 prove this position.

Mid-tribulationists do agree with the scriptures of 1 Thessalonians 4 and Revelation 3:10 as definite passages on the rapture like the Pre-tribulationists. They further point to Revelation 7:14 as proving the Believers spoken of have come out of the Great Tribulation. However Mid-tribulationists believe, it is the Great Tribulation of the last 3½ years that the promise is made to the Church that it will not experience its devastating events.

Some Mid-tribulationists, say there are two scrolls spoken of in the book of Revelation. The scroll of chapter five and its seven seals and the little scroll of Revelation chapter 10 which represents the second half of the Tribulation Period. The first scroll describes the signs and the second describes the events of the end, in Revelation chapters 10 to 22. The first scroll, will begin the Tribulation Period. It will include the suffering of the church and the lost. This will encompass the first 3 ½ years of the Tribulation Period. Then the events of the last 3 ½ years will begin

The scriptures, which support the Mid-Tribulation viewpoint of when the rapture occurs in the Old Testament, are: Joel 2:10, 3:15-16, 3:30-31; Zechariah 1:14-18; Exodus chapters 10 to 22; Daniel 7:13-14, 7:25, 9:27, 11:31, 12:1-2, 12:11; Amos 9:13-15; and Micah 4:1-8. In the New Testament: Matthew 24:7, 9-31; Mark 13:7-27; Luke 21:9-28; 1 Corinthians 15:51; 1 Thessalonians 4:16-17; 2 Thessalonians 2:3-4; and Revelation 4-22.

Mid-Tribulationists point out that 2 Thessalonians 2:7-8 does not necessarily signify the Holy Spirit is totally removed for the entire Tribulation Period. Also, we must be aware of the fact if anyone is to receive salvation during the 70th week, the Holy Spirit according to scripture, would have to necessarily be there for such an event.

Who is the Church and will all the Church be in the Rapture?

According to Mid-Tribulationists even though none of the cardinal scriptures regarding the Rapture mentions the Church, the Church is the subject of those scriptures. They point to the fact that salvation will be no different in the Tribulation Period than it is now. As Believers are a part of the Church now so will they be then.

The Mid-tribulationist believes the Church is promised tribulation and by its worldliness demands it needs to be purged and purified.

The Mid-Tribulation belief is there will be sufficient numbers of people who will become saved during those 3½ years of the Great Tribulation to adequately populate the millennium.

How long are the Tribulation/Great Tribulation Periods?

Mid-tribulationists who believe the Church is raptured at the middle of the Tribulation Period, the question becomes when does the exact middle of the Tribulation Period occur? Some say Revelation chapters 5 through 9 of the scroll represent the first 3½ years and

Revelation 10 through 22, the little scroll represent the second 3½ years.

Others say the first 3½ years of the Tribulation Period encompasses all of Revelation 6:12 – 14:15. This refers to the wrath of man or Satan, which is not as severe as that of God, the second 3 ½ years, which is poured out from Revelation 14:16 – 18:24.

The second half is the Great Tribulation. Another variation of the Mid-Tribulation viewpoint is the book of Revelation never speaks specifically of a seven-year Tribulation Period. Therefore, there are Mid-tribulationists who have made distinction between Daniels 70th Week and the Tribulation Period. **In this regard they say there is no seven-year Tribulation Period. Instead, there is only a 3½ year Tribulation Period.**

When does the wrath of God begin and how long does it last?

Mid-tribulationists believe, regarding the wrath of God, it occurs only during the Great Tribulation. The first 3 ½ years is the wrath of man and the last 3 ½ years is the wrath of God. Some of them believe the wrath of God begins with the pouring out of the vials (interpreted vials in the KJV and Bowls in the NKJV), which occurs in Revelation chapter 16.

When does the Rapture occur according to this viewpoint?

The fact there is a great change to the extent and the harshness of the tribulation in the sixth seal in chapter 6 of Revelation, leading to the Great Tribulation, is the true marker of the Mid-70th Week Rapture. Most Mid-tribulationists believe that the rapture occurs before the seventh seal is opened at Revelation 7:9, 14.

> After these things I looked, and behold, a great multitude which no one could number, of all nations, tribes, peoples, and tongues, standing before the throne and before the Lamb .... "These are the ones who come out of the great tribulation and washed their robes and made them white in the blood of the Lamb."

Others are divided between the sounding of the seventh trumpet, Revelation 11:15 and the angel with the proclamation, Revelation 14:7, as the signal for the Rapture.

What do opposing viewpoints have to say regarding the Mid-Tribulation Rapture?

Pre-tribulationists make a point that the Mid-tribulationists in giving their viewpoint leave out scriptures that point to the exemption of Believers from the Tribulation Period. They say Mid-Tribulation as a compromise between Pre- and Post-Tribulation, which causes it to be a better theory than Post-Tribulation but yet and still is a weaker position than that of the Pre-Tribulation theory.

The Post-tribulationists point to the fact the assertion of the Mid-tribulationists that a time interval is necessary, as 1 and 2 Thessalonians appear to suggest, is not supported by scriptural evidence, therefore, a Post-Tribulation position is more suitable. They disagree with the Mid-Tribulation view the first half of the Tribulation Period represents the wrath of man leaving the second half as the Great Tribulation. They say that Revelation 14:14-16 indicates a Post-Tribulation Rapture event.

CHAPTER FIVE

THE POST-TRIBULATION RAPTURE VIEWPOINT

Post-tribulationists believe that there is nothing in scripture regarding the Tribulation Period that requires the removal of the church. Also, regarding the Second Coming of Jesus Christ/Yeshua HaMashiach there are no scriptures that would not endorse a Post-Tribulation rapture. Fundamentally, the Post-Tribulation viewpoint believes the rapture occurs on the very last day of the seven-year Tribulation Period. They also believe this last day also involves the return of the Lord to conquer the nations at the battle of Armageddon.

The Scriptural Basis for Post-Tribulation Rapture

The Post-Tribulationists feel the following scriptures confirm a Post-Tribulation Rapture: 1) John 14:3 which points to Jesus' going to prepare a place for us and returning and receiving us to Himself. 2) 1 Corinthians 15:51, 52 scriptures refer to the resurrection of the Old Testament Believers/Saints as well as the New Testament Believers along with all that are alive and remain who are caught up to meet the Lord in the air. The Jews of the Old Testament and the Church Believers are caught up together, which would be proof there cannot be two separate events involving the Church and the Jews. 3) In 1 Thessalonians 4:13-18 the Apostle Paul is trying to comfort the Thessalonians with the fact the rapture had not happened at that point and primarily the comfort was to reassure them the dead Believers would be raptured/caught up also. This passage refers to the *"last"* trumpet which would make the event Post-Tribulation. The Greek word for meeting the Lord in the air is a word used for going out to meet visiting dignitaries and accompanying them to their destination, which would explain the "yo-yo" effect of the Post-Tribulation Rapture event.

Here are seven scripture passages for the Post-Tribulation Rapture. Matthew 24:29-31; Luke 17:26-31; 2 Peter 3:8-15; 1 Corinthians 15:50-55; 1 Thessalonians 4:15-17; 2 Thessalonians 1:5-10; 2 Thessalonians 2:1-3. 1 Thessalonians 4:17 is the only scripture that mentions the rapture. A supporting scripture for the 1 Thessalonians 4:17 scripture is Matthew 24:27-31 that specifically states the rapture occurs after the tribulation.

> Immediately after the tribulation of those days the sun will be darkened, and the moon will not give its light; the stars will fall from heaven, and the powers of the heavens will be shaken. Matthew 24:29

1 Corinthians 15:52 agrees with I Thessalonians 4:17 because both passages speak of the last trump. The fact Paul speaks of the last trump they equate with being at the end of the Period. Moreover, the fact is the resurrection of Believers is mentioned in both scriptures. In the 2

Thessalonians 1:8 passage, Paul is stating God will be giving the Believers rest when Jesus/Yeshua returns. They use Luke 17:26-31 to confirm the flood in Noah's day and their entering into the ark all occurred on the same day, which proves a Post-Tribulation Rapture.

Post-Tribulationists render the Greek word "apentesis" interpreted in the narrow sense of meeting the Lord and escorting Him at the *"Parousia," (Coming),* to the earth at that point in time. That is, to escort Him on the last little portion of His descent to earth at the Second Coming.

Who will make up the Church taken in the Rapture?

The Church comprises all true born-again Believers in Jesus Christ/Yeshua HaMashiach from the beginning of recorded history. All Saints/Believers, whether Old Testament, New Testament, or Tribulation Believers are part of the body of Jesus Christ/Yeshua HaMashiach. If they are the Body of Christ/HaMashiach then they are the Church. Ellen Kavanaugh, a Post-Tribulation Messianic Believer explains it is less the Church than it is the commonwealth of Israel. She says Gentiles are grafted into Israel. She believes all who believe in Jesus/Yeshua are part of the elect and they will be those who are raptured after the Tribulation Period.

How long are the Tribulation/Great Tribulation Periods?

The Post-tribulationists believe the analogy of Noah and the flood to the Tribulation Period and the Lord telling him the flood would begin in seven days points to a Post-Tribulation Rapture. Because the flood began seven days *after* the Lord told him to enter the ark the analogy of the rapture would appropriately come at the end of the seven-year Tribulation Period.

The Post-tribulationists believe the end of the anti-Christ's reign precedes the Second Coming of Jesus Christ/Yeshua HaMashiach. They believe the 3½ years preceding the end of the Tribulation Period is the **wrath of the anti-Christ** (Satan) which is the Great Tribulation and occurs just before the Second Coming of the Lord. Although they believe the Church Believers will be in the Great Tribulation and will experience very tough times, they do not believe they will experience the wrath of God. They will be under God's grace.

When does the wrath of God begin and how long does it last?

Post-tribulationists believe the Day of the Lord will not begin until after the Great Tribulation at the end of the Tribulation Period. They believe the wrath of God does not begin until the vials in Revelation 16:2-16. This comes when the nations' armies begin to invade Israel, at the time of Armageddon. In all actuality, the Post-tribulationists believe the Wrath of God, the rapture and the Second Coming of Christ all happen on the same day. This Day of the Lord, the Post-Tribulationists believe will be the very last day of the Tribulation Period. First there will be a resurrection of the dead in Christ/HaMashiach. Second there will be the rapture of those who are alive in Christ/HaMashiach and remain. Third, and finally, the raptured Believers will join the Lord in the air and return with Him to the earth to participate with Him at Armageddon.

When does the Rapture occur according to this viewpoint?

The rapture, according to Post-tribulationists, while the actual word is not stated in scripture the concept of it does occur at the end of the seven-year tribulation period. They say it is tied to the Resurrection at the last day of the Tribulation Period. The rapture of the Church of both Jews and Gentiles shall occur after the Great Tribulation, which is the wrath of Satan, just before the wrath of God and the battle of Armageddon. The rapture occurs at Revelation 14:14-16 when the Son of Man reaps the earth, acknowledging the Son of Man is Jesus Christ/Yeshua HaMashiach.

> Then I looked, and behold, a white cloud, and on the cloud sat One like the Son of Man, having on His head a golden crown, and in His hand a sharp sickle. And another angel came out of the temple, crying with a loud voice to Him who sat on the cloud, "Thrust in Your sickle and reap, for the time has come for You to reap, for the harvest of the earth is ripe." So, He who sat on the cloud thrust in His sickle on the earth, and the earth was reaped. Revelation 14:14-16

The Lord will rapture the Church on His way to Armageddon. In 1 Corinthians 15:51-54 the Apostle Paul explains the rapture by saying all will not sleep but will be raised at the last trump. All those who did not receive the mark of the Beast who survive to the end of the Great Tribulation will be raptured.

What do opposing viewpoints have to say regarding the Post-Tribulation Rapture?

Pre-tribulationists argue the wrath of God spans the entire scroll of Revelation chapter 5, which the seals thereon are opened one by one by the Lamb of God and would make all of the judgments therefore divine.

The Pre and Mid-tribulationists say the *"yo-yo"* effect of going up to meet the Lord and coming directly back down to enter into engagement with non-Believers is implausible and minimizes the importance of the rapture event. They say that Post-Tribulation rapture does not allow time for rewards to be given out.

The Mid-Tribulationists say that Post-Tribulationists cannot explain the tribulation Believers of Revelation 7:9-14.

CHAPTER SIX

MY CONCLUSION AND ANALYSIS OF THE THREE VIEWS OF THE RAPTURE

Before delving into my conclusion and analysis I would like to reiterate no point of view of a single event can completely and adequately address the rapture of the church. There is nowhere in scripture a statement that actually states *this is the rapture and it shall occur at this particular time.*

The resolution is there is **more than one event and until the Church comes to that realization,** the rapture will not be able to be reconciled.

The Controversy

The great majority of the Church, I believe, agrees there will be a rapture of the Church. It is generally accepted there will only be one rapture of the Church, although there are multiple examples of rapture events in the Bible. The controversy comes over when that event will take place: whether before the Tribulation Period, as the Pre-tribulationists believe; during the Tribulation Period, according to the Mid-tribulationists; or whether after the Tribulation Period, as the Post-tribulationists say. All of these viewpoints agree the Believers will not undergo the wrath of God, although there is disagreement as to what is and when the wrath of God is applied.

Finally, there is controversy over who is taken out of the world as the *"Church"* and who is left.

Who is the Church?

Most Pre-tribulationists say the Church, which is not mentioned in the book of Revelation after chapter 3, is not present in the Tribulation Period. This they say is because true Believers who are a part of what we think of as the organized Church of Believers, (denominations and non-denominations) are taken out in the first event of the rapture. However, the Mid-Tribulationists believe the event will not occur until the middle of the Tribulation Period and assert newly saved Believers (Messianic and Christian) are included and become a part of the body of Christ during the Tribulation Period, and therefore are a part of the Church. We know there are saved people in the Tribulation Period because the book of Revelation chapter 7:14 says a great multitude of Believers/Saints came out of "the" Great Tribulation. In addition, Revelation chapter 14 which is deep into the Tribulation Period speaks of the people of God who did not take the mark of the beast will be blessed if they die in the Lord, Revelation 14:13-16. The Post-Tribulation Believers use this scripture as their point of rapture. Therefore, the Church consists of all saved Believer/Saints and they will participate in the catching away.

How long are the Tribulation/Great Tribulation Periods?

The Pre-Tribulation viewpoint is the Tribulation Period is the entire seven years of Daniel 9:27. The Mid-Tribulation viewpoint has disagreement within its ranks, some say seven years, others say 3 ½ years. Many Mid-tribulationists even disagree as to how they are labeled, Mid-tribulationists, pre-wrath or mid-seventieth week. Post-tribulationists also disagree within their ranks regarding the length of the Tribulation Period. The question of whether the Great Tribulation differs from the overall period and if so what length does it comprise, enters the controversy. **What the research has shown** is the Pre-tribulationists hold, of course, to an event prior to the Tribulation Period, but differ regarding the Great Tribulation; some believe it is the entire period while others say it is the last 3½ years. The Mid-tribulationists point to the mid-point of the Tribulation Period as the beginning but differ as to when the Great Tribulation occurs in the book of Revelation. The Post-Tribulation advocates say the Great Tribulation occurs on the last day of the Tribulation Period.

For the sake of clarity, I will make a table of scriptures pertaining to this period of seven years. From this table we can perhaps determine the length of the Great Tribulation whether or not it coincides with the seven-year treaty or a different specified length of time. We know there are time periods spoken of as a time, times and half a time, 42 months and also 1260 days all of which are 3 ½ years on the Biblical calendar. From information in the table below, we can determine how many times they occur and in which context are they mentioned.

Of the scriptures listed in the table below which have an influence on the timing of the seven-year tribulation period, only the book of Daniel 12:7 tells us how long the Great tribulation is, for it refers back to verse one:

> And there shall be a time of trouble, such as never was since there was a nation, even to that time. And at that time your people shall be delivered, everyone who is found written in the book. Daniel 12:1b

Then verse seven tells us:

> Then I heard the man clothed in linen, who was above the waters of the river, when he held up his right hand and his left hand to heaven, and swore by Him who lives forever, that it shall be for a time, times and half a time; and when the power of the holy people has been completely shattered, all these things shall be finished. Daniel 12:7

Table I

Scriptures Pertaining to the Great Tribulation

Time, times ½ time	42 months	1260 days	Context of Scripture
Daniel 7:25			Believers are given into the hands of the anti-Christ
Daniel 12:7			How long is the time of trouble & its fulfillment?
	Revelation 11:2		Gentiles tread holy city underfoot
		Revelation 11:3	The two witnesses prophesy
		Revelation 12:6	Israel flees into the wilderness
Revelation 12:14			The woman on two wings of an eagle
	Revelation 13:5		The beast is given authority to continue 42 months

The scripture above tells us all things shall be finished after 3½ years. Therefore, to be finished the 3½ years will have to coordinate with end of the Tribulation Period. This is the only scripture that actually mentions a time period for all things to be finished, which gives us the end of the Tribulation Period. Therefore, the Great Tribulation shall be for a time, times, and half a time, which would be 3½ years. Now since the Great Tribulation is 3½ years, then it cannot extend the entire seven years of the treaty signed by the anti-Christ/HaMashiach.

When does the wrath of God begin and how long does it last?

There is the view of some Pre-tribulationists that say the wrath of God begins with the opening of the seals beginning in Revelation 6:1, because the opening of the seals occurs in the throne of God and represents His divine wrath or judgment. Others say at the opening of the sixth seal at Revelation 6:12. Mid-tribulationists disagree anywhere from Revelation 6:17 to Revelation 14:17 and the grapes of wrath. Now the viewpoint of the Post-tribulationists, who say the Great Tribulation is not the wrath of God but the wrath of Satan, complicates the controversy. Their position is on the last day of the Tribulation Period with the bowl judgments of chapter 16 of the book of Revelation God pours out His wrath. The wrath of God, they say, the rapture and the Second Coming of Christ/HaMashiach all occur on that last day (Armstrong).

What are the problems with the three viewpoints?

The problem the **Pre-tribulationists** have is to explain salvation in the Tribulation Period. Their resolution is to have those who receive salvation go through the Tribulation Period and then directly into the millennium (the 1,000-year reign of Jesus Christ/Yeshua HaMashiach) and be those who are ruled in the millennium (Strandberg, Def. Pre-Trib). They have this problem because they say all nations are destroyed at Armageddon. The **Mid-tribulationists** say the Church goes through the first half of the Tribulation, which is not the wrath of God, then they are raptured. Those left behind and become Believers will be sufficient to populate the millennium. They too, believe all nations are destroyed at Armageddon. They recognize Church Believers will go through some tribulation but not the Great Tribulation, which is the wrath of God during the rule of the anti-Christ/HaMashiach in the second half of the Tribulation Period (121-22). The prime belief of the **Post-tribulationists** is the Church will go through the entire Tribulation Period. They will be raptured on the last day and will meet the Lord in the air and return with Him on His descent at His Second Coming to destroy the nations at Armageddon (Finley, The Post-Tribulation Rapture). All three viewpoints believe the battle of Armageddon destroys all nations and peoples (Kelley). This position is difficult for all three viewpoints to explain according to their theory. In the final analysis, what they have in common is the view there is only one event, which will remove all Believers from the earth at their particular viewpoint's occurrence.

Therefore, we have an all-out attempt by each to disapprove the other two viewpoints in order to have their viewpoint be the only true and accepted viewpoint. In each, there are those who are very adamant in their position and those who admit one cannot give an adequate exegesis of the rapture (Archer 144-45; Moo 89-90, 211; Stanton Ch. 9).

Though we cannot pinpoint exactly when these signs and events begin or end, we can put them in an order, which can give us enough information so we can be comforted and assured as to what is on the agenda of God the Father, God the Son and God the Holy Spirit. Now, that is exactly what I will do in my reconciliation in the next chapter.

CHAPTER SEVEN

MY RECONCILIATION OF THE TRI-TRIBULATION RAPTURE

The Justification according to God's plan

For all people who have and will choose to receive God and to make Him the Lord of their lives, God has provided a way of departure from this world into His presence prior to His return. The escape from this world is to have eternal life with the Lord and not eternal damnation in Hell. There are many examples in chapter 2 regarding many instances of God providing an escape valve, as it were, for those that chose to follow/obey God. Among these, I gave examples of people who escaped through being raptured: Enoch, Elijah, Paul and John. God chose to do a supernatural feat for these people and He has made a promise to those of us who are alive just before His Second Advent, to catch us up to Himself in the air and to forever be with Him, 1 Thessalonians 4:17. Jesus Christ/Yeshua HaMashiach Himself chose the Apostle Paul to give the gospel message to the Gentiles. In our scripture reference above, Paul has stated to us through his letter to the Thessalonians the Lord will rapture (catch) us up to Himself in two phases. First, the dead will rise. Second, those who remain and are alive will be caught up to meet Him in the clouds. Therefore, each rapture event will involve these two phases, which are, by the way, instantaneous. The rapture of the dead and those who are alive in Christ/HaMashiach shall meet Him in the clouds.

I am not going to present an argument to persuade the reader at this point there will be a rapture. I have presented that argument in chapter 1 and 2, here I assume the reader is convinced there is or at the least has a curiosity as to how the Tri-Tribulation Rapture can be reconciled. What I will do is to present scriptures for each event and apply them to that event. There are several mentions of lengths of time in scripture concerning the Tribulation Period. Each of these lengths of time has some bearing on the Tribulation period. Therefore, I have gathered this information and developed a timetable, which shows how each interacts with the others. **With the pertinent scriptures and the timetable, it will be possible to explain when, the approximate points, God intends to take His people out of this world shall occur.**

There are many subtle points that need to be explained which will tie together the three events of the Tri-Tribulation Rapture. The Lord said no one knows the day or the hour of His coming (Matthew 24:36). This, of course, applies to His coming to rapture/catch us away as well as His Second Coming to rule and reign upon the earth. However, once we have the correct interpretation of the scriptures we can then feel more comfortable and confident about our future. In addition, when the Tri-Tribulation Rapture begins, there will be comfort and hope for those who will not be a part of the first event. After all, there will be more events to come.

This is a good place to point out what exactly takes place at the rapture in regard to the three components that make up the individual, our spirit, soul and body (1 Thessalonians 5:23). The Bible says when we die, fall asleep as the Apostle Paul puts it, our spirit goes back to God to whom it belongs and the physical body returns to the dust from which it was made (Ecclesiastes 12:7). The soul, which consists of the mind, will and emotions is what differentiates us from one another. The soul is the everlasting consciousness, which will spend its eternity either in the Kingdom of God or in outer darkness/Hell/the lake of fire (Matthew 10:28, 25:30, Revelation 20:15).

The saved soul goes to heaven along with the spirit. The soul and the spirit are the true person. In heaven, they are recognizable as the person who was on the earth before death and housed on earth in their earthly, physical body. They are perfect and young, the reason for that is 33 was the age of Jesus at His resurrection and He has imputed *"we shall be like Him"* (1 John 3:2). The soul that is "not saved" will be separated from the spirit and is cast into Hell until the judgment and then into the lake of fire for all eternity (Mark 8:36, Matthew 10:28, Revelation 20:15). Now the body which has expired or been destroyed is in the grave or place where it was destroyed, for example by fire, drowning, or as ashes, even because of cremation or war. The Apostle Paul tells us in the book of 1 Thessalonians 4:13-18 when Jesus Christ/Yeshua HaMashiach comes to rapture the Church the dead in Christ/HaMashiach **will rise first to meet Him in the air**. Well if the person is a spirit with a soul and is in heaven when the event occurs and he or she has a heavenly body, how is it the earthly remains (physical body in the grave) rises to meet Jesus\Yeshua in the clouds? The explanation is this: Jesus created us a tripartite being and wants us to regain our three components. Therefore, **the body that is in heaven is a form of a spiritual body but not our final glorified, immortal, body**. As we know, Jesus/Yeshua resurrected into a spiritual and glorified body, which was able to pass through walls and yet eat food with the disciples (Luke 24:34-42). We know He came in a glorified body because there has been no evidence of Jesus' earthly remains after His resurrection, therefore, in order to pass through walls His physical body had to have changed. Jesus/Yeshua told the disciples He was not a spirit (ghost) because He had flesh and bones. So those who are in heaven in a spiritual body when Jesus summons their physical body, from their graves, see Ezekiel 37:1-14, Matthew 27:51-53, **to unite the spiritual person with their physical bodies, they must come from heaven with Jesus. That will be at the instant He comes to meet in the air (clouds) those caught up and changed into glorified immortal bodies**. The Apostle explains to us in the book of 1 Corinthians 15:42-58 the difference between the natural and spiritual bodies. In verse 53 it says, **"For this corruptible must put on incorruption and this mortal must put on immortality."**

Length of the Tribulation Period

To begin my reconciliation of The Tri-Tribulation rapture, having established there will be one or more rapture events, it is necessary to start with the establishment of the time period within which the rapture(s) will occur. The book of Daniel 9:27 establishes that time with the signing of the peace treaty (covenant) by the prince (who is the man of sin, and the anti-Christ). The verse tells us the time is one week of years, seven years. That establishes the length of the Tribulation/Great Tribulation periods. In Daniel chapter 9, the fact is, each week in the weeks of years is seven years and confirmed by the crucifixion of Jesus Christ/Yeshua HaMashiach. From the command to restore Jerusalem until the death of Messiah the Prince would be 483 years or 69 weeks of years, which Jesus Christ/Yeshua HaMashiach fulfilled (Haggai chapter 1). Therefore, the Tribulation Period is seven years, because it is stated in Daniel 9:27 *"Then he shall confirm a covenant with many for one week,"* and there is only one week left to yet be fulfilled of the 70 weeks in Daniel chapter 9. Jesus/Yeshua confirmed in Matthew 24:15 when He referred to this very verse to let us know the fulfillment of it had not occurred and was yet future and is in fact a truth that must occur.

Chronology of the book of Revelation

Revelation chapters 6 to 19 are an exegesis of the Tribulation Period. In order to reconcile properly the rapture, we must establish when in the chronology of the seals on the scroll of Revelation chapter 6 does the Tribulation period begin and when does the Great Tribulation and/or the wrath of God begin if indeed they are different and occur at different points in time. Once established we must draw a correlation as to when the rapture events occur.

From Revelation 6:1 to 22:21 the book is about the things, which must happen in the future. This includes the entire Church Age, the Tribulation Period, the Millennial Reign of Christ/HaMashiach, the Judgment seat, and the New Earth and Kingdom of God. Starting in chapter 4 John translated into the throne room of God views the entire future of heaven and earth until the Kingdom of God arrives in the New Earth. What we must understand in reading through the chapters of the book of Revelation is some of the time we have a glimpse of what is going on in heaven and some of the time what is going to happen to the earth and all who dwell thereon. This tends to make us have to change perspectives as to whether we are looking from the Spiritual standpoint of heaven or from the natural aspect of what the effect the seals opened have upon the earth.

If we look closely at the chapters of Revelation beginning in chapter 6, we can separate the chapters along these lines:

- Chapter 6 – The Lamb begins to open the seals of the scroll. The first six seals until chapter 6 verse 12 are the benchmarks of the Church Age from John until, according to Pre-tribulationists, the Day of the Lord, the Wrath of God. What we find in Revelation 6:1-11 are seals one through five, the church age up until the Tribulation Period, which would include the treaty signed by the anti-Christ. The **sixth** seal starting at verse 12 is about the disruption and disturbances in the environment involving the entire earth. We have read these events in other chapters of the Bible that would be included in the Last Days. The sun becomes black like sackcloth, the moon becomes like blood, stars fall, mountains and islands move out of place like in earthquakes, etcetera, as in the book of Isaiah, the book of Joel, the book of Mathew and the book of Mark. The important thing to note here is in verse 17 it says, *"For the great day of His wrath has come, and who is able to stand?"* Also, note there is no mention yet about the arrival of a person among the nations who will sign a treaty for seven years, but then again it does not say one has not come. The end of the sixth seal ends with this declaration:

> Fall on us and hide us from the face of Him who sits on the throne and from the wrath of the Lamb! For the great day of His wrath has come and who is able to stand? Revelation 6:16-17

But does this declare the beginning of the tribulation which Jesus/Yeshua spoke of in Matthew 24:21 or as the above verse 17 seems to imply tribulation was progressively getting worse and this declaration occurs somewhere in the middle of the Tribulation Period. Being there is no mention as to the length of days before this declaration is made gives some room as to when it occurs exactly.

- Chapter 7 – There is a pause in the effects of the seals as the seventh seal is about to be opened. In chapter 7, the 144,000 are sealed in their foreheads from the 12 tribes of Israel. Revelation 7:9-14 is a hiatus to allow for a great multitude coming out of the Great Tribulation. Is this great multitude, at this point, already raptured prior to the Tribulation Period, before the first 3½ years or are they raptured in the middle of the Tribulation Period? Many of the Mid-tribulationists believe they have been raptured now at what they believe is the mid-point of the Tribulation Period. If in fact these are raptured in the middle, then these could not be the same Believers of Revelation 5:9-11 as the Pre-tribulationist believes. Of course there is a question whether these in chapter 5 are Church age Believers or are they Believers of the Old Testament/Tenakh since John was raptured/caught up before the seals were opened and the first through fifth seal has to do with what is to happen during the Church age before the treaty of Daniel 9:27. Revelation 5:9-11 Believers could not be Believers from the beginning of the Church Age, Acts 2:4 until Revelation 6:12. Because chapter 7 is a pause in the action of the seven seals, that is, before we get to the seventh seal, then we can take it this is an expository (informative) chapter. It is showing us the Believers were Raptured before the Great Tribulation, which may or may not include both the Pre-Tribulation and Mid-Tribulation Rapture events.

- Chapter 8 – We return to the seals at the seventh seal and it says, "there was silence in heaven for about half an hour," Revelation 8:1. This is as though things are on hold for a short time. If we look at half an hour biblically from God's perspective then we find it is considerably longer than a half an hour in the natural scheme of things for man. Since the angel said about a half an hour, if we estimate it may be a bit more or less than six weeks or a month and a half reckoning a thousand years is as a day to the Lord (2 Peter 3:8).

This allows the seven angels, which are to sound the seven trumpets, time for them to prepare. Then an angel takes a censor, fills it with the prayers of the Believers, and offers them upon the altar, then "filled it with fire from the altar and threw it to the earth. And there were noises, thundering and an earthquake" (Revelation 8:5), this is what happened during the half an hour while the seven angels prepared to sound. Then the angels with the seven trumpets begin to sound beginning at Revelation 8:7-12, which gives us the terrible devastation that occurs over one-third of earth's surface and atmosphere. The first four trumpets have an effect on one-third of the earth in some aspect, whether it is on life, vegetation, ships, night, day and even man himself. This could very well be the effects of all-out nuclear war. If so then these trumpets would very likely have to sound simultaneously. Perhaps the apparent separation of the first four trumpets from the fifth and sixth trumpets here indicates the first four are perhaps simultaneous actions. Most likely, the first four trumpets herald the beginning of the Great Tribulation.

Developing a Tribulation Period Timetable

The reason for the timetable is **there are many lengths of time within the seven-year tribulation period the Lord has given us which must be reconciled and explained** in terms of the possibility of a rapture event or events occurring: before, during, at the end of or at a particular time or sub-period.

As has been discussed previously, **the major problem** with the single event rapture theory, it is **one single event to the exclusion of any other possibility. Well, this presentation reconciles the separate viewpoints into one** homogeneous workable plan for the Lord Jesus Christ/Yeshua HaMashiach to take His people out of this perverse, sin-sick world. Not that this treatise will be the exact scenario the Lord will use, but **we can understand the greater possibility is there are three events and not one.** The exact timing as the Bible tells us is in God's hands not ours. Therefore, it is my contention there will be Pre-Tribulation, Mid-Tribulation, and Post-Tribulation Rapture events. After you have read this presentation, you will agree three events is the only acceptable explanation of rapture that encompasses all of scripture. You will see, after all, God is not the author of confusion and **all scriptures given in reference to a particular rapture rightly fit together forming *The Tri-Tribulation Rapture of the Church.***

In order to complete, the timetable the informational items need to be gathered which will give the answers needed for The Tri-Tribulation Rapture. The following scriptures will give us pieces of information given by God in order to develop a timetable, they are:

- Daniel 8:13, 14 – end of daily sacrifice – the transgression of desolation – sanctuary and host to be trampled underfoot for 2300 days and the sanctuary will be cleansed

- Daniel 9:25 – 69 weeks

- Daniel 9:27 – covenant – seven years – the end of sacrifice and offerings in the middle of the seven years

- Daniel 12:1 – Will be a time of trouble such as never was. All Israel, in the book of Life, shall be saved

- Daniel 12:7 – Jesus/Yeshua says it will be for a time, times and half a time, 3½ years and it will be finished (the fulfillment) – when the power of the holy people has been completely shattered

- Daniel 12:11 – time from the daily sacrifice taken away until the abomination of desolation is 1290 days

- Daniel 12:12 – Blessed is he who waits and comes to the 1335th day

- Matthew 24:15 – Therefore when you see the abomination of desolation

- Revelation 13:5 – the beast is given authority for 42 months

- Revelation 16:17 – "It is done!"

- Revelation 19:20 – the beast was captured, and with him the false prophet

With the above, we shall put together a timetable from which we will be able to explain The Tri-Tribulation Rapture.

First, let us look at some numbers in relation to the Tribulation Period so we have the correct perspective as we delve into The Tri-Tribulation Rapture. We know the treaty signed is for 2520 days, seven years, based on the

Biblical reckoning of a year being 360 days. However, we must take into account since the days Jesus/Yeshua walked the earth the calendar for the great majority of the world has been the Gregorian calendar of 365 days in the year. However, in Judaism a month added periodically makes up the difference. There still appears to be a discrepancy in the computation from one calendar to the other. From the position of the Post-Tribulation viewpoint, the rapture will occur at least the specified number of days regardless of which calendar is used. Because they say the resurrection, the rapture, the wrath of God and the Second Advent all happen on the last day of the Tribulation Period. It certainly does not complicate the calculation of when that would be on either calendar. It is necessary to point out some points for those who hold a very strict interpretation of the rapture. **We must acknowledge God can fulfill the rapture and not have it occur in the exact timing we give Him to perform it/them.** As for the Mid-Tribulation Rapture, it can occur in a myriad of points in time within the Tribulation Period, as discussed in chapter 2. The Mid-Tribulation Rapture event can happen any time that is closer to the mid-point of the seven years than to either end of the period. This could mean anytime from the 631st day to the 1889th day after the signing of the treaty or covenant the Mid-Tribulation Rapture could occur and still be within the concept of being in the middle. According to my reconciliation and according to the scriptures the Mid-Tribulation Rapture will not occur in the *"exact middle"* of the Tribulation Period.

When we are trying to discern, apply and explain what God is saying in His Word we must understand God is omni-dimensional in every aspect, while we are three-dimensional at best. Most of us when interpreting the Word of God apply the Word in a linear and chronological order. However, if we take but a minute, for those of us who have read the Bible cover to cover, we understand God does not follow a linear and chronological order in giving us the events that occur in His Word. He even tells us in His Word He knows the end from the beginning. God is omni-directional, that is, He can travel in any direction and be in any place at the same time, if we can imagine it, He has already been there and is there. If we can think of it, He has already done it and is doing it. In beginning, before creating anything, all was in Him. How He chose to begin was already in Him. Therefore, light, dark, elements, and substance were already within Him. When He began, it was not in a linear fashion but omni-dimensional and omni-directional. This may sound chaotic and confusing, but while we look at the things of God in a linear and chronological fashion, God performs in an omnidimensional, omnidirectional and omnipresent fashion. That is why there are so many sevens in the book of Revelation, because God in order to give us an inkling of what and how He does things He has to give us His works from so many directions or explanations that we with our linear perspective might begin to discern the truth of what He has done. In the case of the number seven and God using it to put in perspective times and seasons along with the order of events, God has made a covenant with the number seven. He has set it apart as His perfect number that announces His completion and perfection of what He has done beginning with creation and following through to Revelation 20:15 which is the Great White

Throne Judgment. At that point, the natural state of humanity will end at the end of the millennial reign of Jesus Christ/Yeshua HaMashiach, which will be the end of the **seventh millennium** from the creation of mankind in the Biblical narrative. Therefore, what we see as events occurring one after the other may be or probably are simultaneous events which when placed one upon the other are congruent (matching). The great example of this are the gospels. They are about the same identical subject but all have a different perspective. It is like a theater full of people watching the same movie and if interviewed separately all would have a different perspective on the same identical subject but there would be enough points all would make regarding the movie so they would be congruent with one another. Therefore, as we look at what God is saying to us concerning the rapture we must allow ourselves a certain amount of flexibility and not hold God to a linear, chronological presentation of the events as they occur. However, for our benefit the events are in a nearly chronological order.

In order that our timetable not get too cluttered and confusing to the reader by putting all the information on the timetable at once. I will add each scripture reference or references that apply one at a time. After all is done for scriptures that pertain to the seven-year Tribulation Period as spoken of in Daniel 9:27, I will then explain The Tri-Tribulation Rapture so it will become clear **this is God's intended plan.**

The periods given in scripture are from the Biblical perspective. Another point to make prior to developing our timetable is information placed on our timetable will be according to the Biblical calendar. I will confine my explanation to the Biblical calendar. Finally, I would like you to **understand the interpretation of specific days, months or years are not to be taken as hard and fast points in time. What we understand is God has a plan, which will accomplish these events: The Pre-Tribulation Rapture; the Mid-Tribulation Rapture**; and **the Post-Tribulation Rapture** to recover His people and perform that which He has promised.

We begin by establishing our baseline from the scripture of Daniel 9:27, *"Then he shall confirm a covenant with many for one week; ...."* If we calculate the 69 weeks (Daniel 9:25) it comes to 483 years by counting each week as seven years. Then we find from the time the command to rebuild the Temple and restore Jerusalem, Haggai 1:1-9, until the death of Jesus Christ/HaMashiach on the cross was 483 years. This leaves one week of seven years left to the prophecy. How do we know the week has not already been fulfilled? First of all, Jesus/Yeshua Himself signaled the completion of the 483 years, therefore, we know the last week of seven years would have to be after His resurrection. Jesus/Yeshua gave us two clues, both in the future, concerning the unfulfilled seven-year week. First in Matthew 24:15 Jesus/Yeshua says, "when you see," referring to the abomination of desolation in Daniel nine 9:27; also, there would be tribulation in the world, greater than ever before seen from the beginning or ever shall be. From the point in time of the "Olivet Discourse" the "when you see" would be a future event. Also, "great tribulation" that has not been, we know it has not occurred because we have already seen greater tribulation than that of the time of the "Olivet Discourse" and as yet the events of the Great Tribulation have not occurred. Therefore, we establish our timetable at seven years. I begin by placing on the timetable the seven-year period in the table below.

Table II
The 70th Week of Daniel 9:27

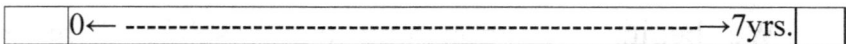

0← --→7yrs.

We will now begin to add information to our baseline according to the scriptures that pertain to this seven-year period as it affects the rapture events. **Because the information given is in days and months as well as years, information will be added in the form given. I will shade newly added information to our timetable as we go.** We know the treaty to sign is for 2520 days, seven years, based on the Biblical reckoning of a year being 360 days. In terms of months, the seven-year period will equal 84 months. I now add this to the timetable.

Table III
Converting Seven Years to Days and Months

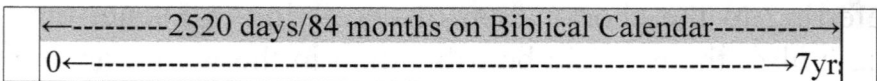

←---------2520 days/84 months on Biblical Calendar---------→
0←---→7yr

Because Daniel 9:27 says in the middle of the week he shall bring an end to sacrifice and offering, I have divided the week into two equal parts of 3½ years each. This is the most likely presumption one would make that the middle means the division of the week is in two equal parts. However, as we will see, this is not likely for other scriptures do not permit fulfilling *"all"* into the two equal periods. Besides, the scripture does not say at the mid-point. It says the middle and middle can mean anywhere from the 631st day until the 1889th day from the confirmation of the covenant for seven years. However, Daniel 12:7 gives us: it will be for a time, times and half a time 3½ years and it will be finished (the fulfillment) – when the power of the holy people has been completely shattered. Therefore, we backtrack 3½ years from the end of the Tribulation Period. The end of sacrifice and offering must be between the 631st day and the 1260th day, 3 ½ years, the exact middle of the Tribulation Period.

I now place this information on the timetable showing how the middle of the week can cover a considerable period of time itself:

Table IV

Middle of the Week Daniel 9:27; 12:7

Mid-point of the 70th Week

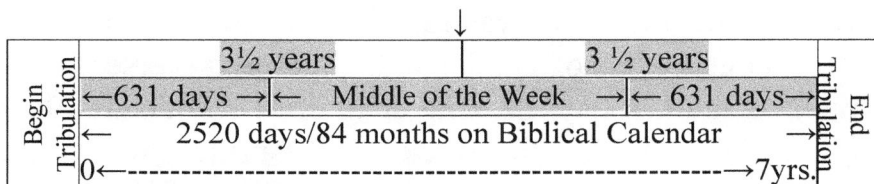

↓

Begin Tribulation	3½ years		3 ½ years	Tribulation End
	←631 days →|←	Middle of the Week	→|← 631 days→	
	←	2520 days/84 months on Biblical Calendar	→	
0←		--	→7yrs.	

Next, he, the prince, the anti-Christ, will bring an end to sacrifice and offering. When does this occur and why be concerned about this? At first glance, it appears not to have any effect on the rapture, but if we consider, it says this happens in the middle of the week and we say there will be a Mid-Tribulation Rapture, is it not possible this could be a signal for the Mid-Tribulation Rapture. Besides, other events are dependent on when the taking away sacrifice and offerings occurs. Let us put it into our timetable.

> He even exalted himself as high as the Prince of the host; and by him the daily sacrifices were taken away, and the place of His sanctuary was cast down. Daniel 8:11

Here in Daniel 8:11 the little horn (the anti-Christ, the beast) will cause the sacrifice and offering to cease. How do we know this is the anti-Christ? Well, if we read verse 9 and 10 it tells us the little horn of Daniel's vision grew up to challenge God and even caused some of the heavenly host to be cast down along with some of the stars, which we know from Revelation 1:20 are angels. Then, if we compare with Revelation 12:4, 7 we see the dragon, the devil, fought with Michael the archangel over Israel and he, the devil, was cast down to earth with a third of the angels. Also, Daniel 8:23 interprets verse 11 by saying in the last days "a king shall arise …" Daniel 9:27 says in the middle of the week he, the prince, will cause the sacrifice and offerings to cease. In chapter 8, it says:

Then I heard a holy one speaking; and another holy one said to that certain one who was speaking, "How long will the vision be, concerning the daily sacrifices and the transgression of desolation, the giving of both the sanctuary and the host to be trampled underfoot?" And he said to me, "For two thousand three hundred days; then the sanctuary shall be cleansed." Daniel 8:13-14

The Lord tells Daniel the length of time is for 2300 days, after which the sanctuary is cleansed. Therefore, if the sanctuary were to be cleansed after the 2300 days the most likely explanation would be it must coincide with Christ's Second Coming to set up His millennial rule, which would then be at the end of the seven-year treaty. The other possibility is it would begin with the treaty, but then it says the sanctuary would be cleansed at the end and that would put us right in the middle of the rule of the anti-Christ who will not cleanse the sanctuary and make it righteous or holy. In fact, he is the one who will desecrate the Holy Place as the abomination of desolations. Therefore, we see from Daniel 8:14 the period in the vision for the daily sacrifice and the transgression of desolation begins at the 220th day after the confirmation of the covenant. Therefore, since we know the order to cease the ritual of sacrifice and offerings in the Temple has to be in the middle of the week, we know it cannot be before the 631st day from the confirmation of the treaty. We are not told what day the sacrifice and offerings will cease only that the prince will cause it to cease. Therefore, we can establish that the 631st day is the earliest possibility for the sacrifice and offerings to cease. So, we can add to the timetable beginning at the 631st day after the signing of the covenant, the first possible day when the practice of sacrifice and offering can be taken away from the Jews in their worship in the Temple which is to be erected and completed prior to this point or even before the Tribulation Period itself. Mind you, I am not suggesting the sacrifices and offerings begin with the signing of the covenant. They could well have started sometime before the signed covenant. We now place the taking away of the sacrifice and offering on our timetable.

What our timetable tells us at this point is the sacrifice and offerings are taken away between the 631st day of the Tribulation Period and the 1889th day in order to satisfy being taken away in the middle of the week.

Table V

The Sacrifice and Offerings Taken Away
Daniel 8:11, 14

Mid-point of the 70th Week

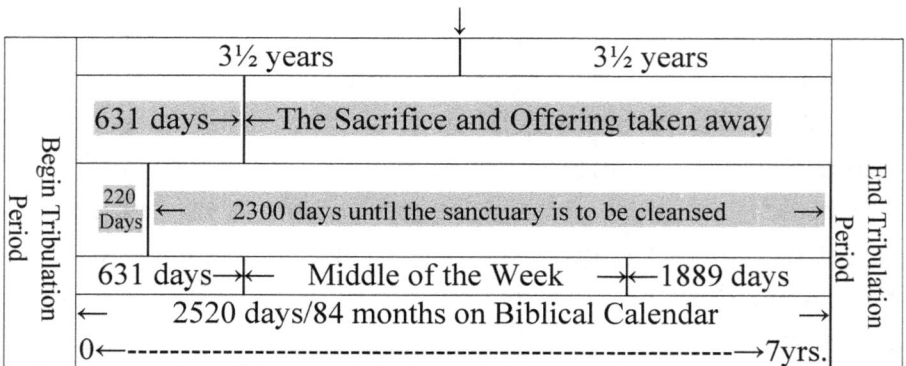

Begin Tribulation Period	3½ years	3½ years	End Tribulation Period
	631 days→ ←The Sacrifice and Offering taken away		
	220 Days ← 2300 days until the sanctuary is to be cleansed →		
	631 days→ ← Middle of the Week → ←1889 days		
	← 2520 days/84 months on Biblical Calendar →		
	0←--→7yrs.		

Daniel 12:11 tells us from the time the daily sacrifice is taken away until the abomination of desolation is set up is 1290 days. Therefore, we can now put in place when the abomination of desolation will be set up, 1290 days after the end of sacrifice and offering. If we add the 1290 days until the abomination of desolation to the 631 days, the earliest day that can occur for the end of the sacrifice and offerings, we will have the abomination of desolation occurring at 1921 days. Then we can say the abomination of desolation will be set up 1921 days after the confirmation of the treaty. Jesus tells us "Therefore when you see the abomination of desolation, spoken of by Daniel the prophet, standing in the holy place (whoever reads, let him understand)," Matthew 24:15. What I believe Jesus is saying is everyone, especially the Jews, must understand this is the anti-Christ beast and you will now need to flee for your life, natural and eternal.

You might ask is this the only possibility for the abomination of desolation? Of course not! This, in my discernment, is the earliest possibility for setting up the abomination of desolation. Now having said that, we need to understand the limiting factors in our information that narrow the possibilities. The fact the abomination of desolation is 1290 days after the taking away of the sacrifice and offerings tells us there needs to be time before the end of the Tribulation Period in order to fulfill the rest of the events of the period.

Table VI

1290 Days until the Abomination of Desolation
Daniel 12:11

Mid-point of the 70th Week

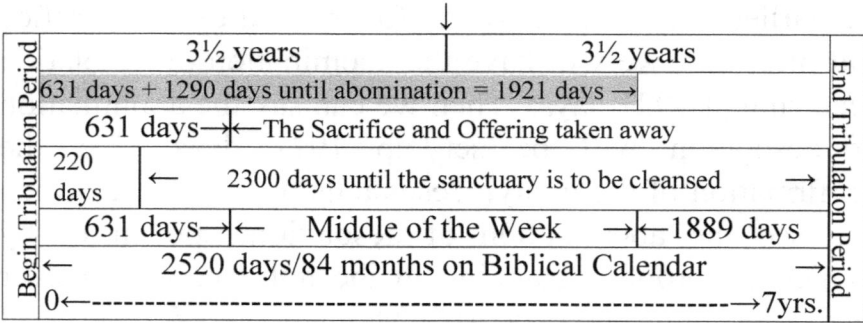

Begin Tribulation Period	3½ years	3½ years	End Tribulation Period
	631 days + 1290 days until abomination = 1921 days →		
	631 days→ ←The Sacrifice and Offering taken away		
	220 days	← 2300 days until the sanctuary is to be cleansed →	
	631 days→ ← Middle of the Week →←1889 days		
	← 2520 days/84 months on Biblical Calendar →		
	0←--→7yrs.		

There is still the fulfilling of the 42 months given to the anti-Christ and the period of 1335 days. In addition, we know the end of sacrifice and offerings must take place in the middle of the week. This limits us to sometime before the exact center of the Tribulation Period.

Up until now, we have built our timetable based on the signing of the treaty of Daniel 9:27. This information is necessary to be able to explain the Pre-Tribulation and Mid-Tribulation Rapture events. In order to explain the Post-Tribulation Rapture event, we will need information relating to the end of the Tribulation Period. In the book of Revelation, it says:

> Then the beast was captured, and with him the false prophet who worked signs in his presence, by which he deceived those who received the mark of the beast and those who

worshiped his image. These two were cast alive into the lake of fire burning with brimstone. Revelation 19:20

Even though the voice from the Temple of heaven in Revelation 16:17 says, *"It is done!"* for our purposes we will take Revelation 19:20 as the finish of all things pertaining to the Tribulation Period and the rapture events.

Daniel 12:7 tells us after a time, times and half a time, 3½ years; all these things shall be finished. In addition, it tells us the power of the holy people shall be shattered. It has to be when all things are finished we will have reached the end of the time of the anti-Christ, the beast, which will be at Revelation 19:20. Also:

In addition, he was given a mouth speaking great things and blasphemies, and he was given authority to continue for forty-two months. Revelation 13:5

Therefore, *"he,"* the anti-Christ/HaMashiach (beast) is given 42 months to continue to reign. If the end of his reign culminates with his capture and being thrown into the Lake of Fire, then we must place the end of his reign at the end of the Tribulation Period and count backward which would be of course at the exact center of the Tribulation Period. By placing the time, which the anti-

Table VII

The Beast is given 42 Months to Continue
Revelation 13:5

Mid-point of the 70th Week

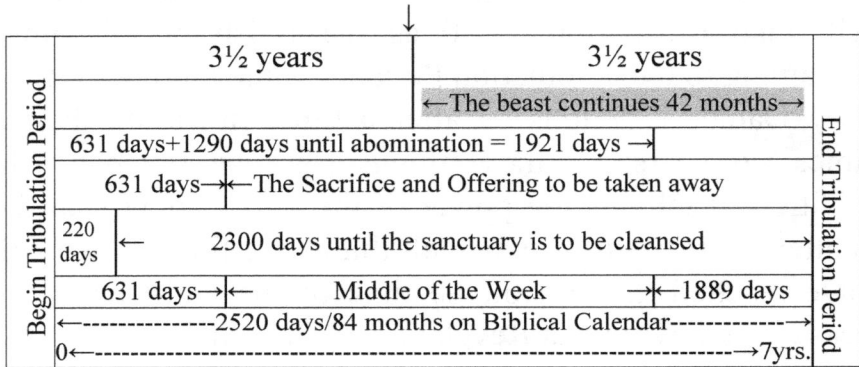

	3½ years	3½ years	
Begin Tribulation Period		←The beast continues 42 months→	End Tribulation Period
	631 days+1290 days until abomination = 1921 days →		
	631 days→ ←The Sacrifice and Offering to be taken away		
	220 days ← 2300 days until the sanctuary is to be cleansed →		
	631 days→ ← Middle of the Week →←1889 days		
	←----------2520 days/84 months on Biblical Calendar----------→		
	0←--→7yrs.		

Christ's rule continues will also give us the time of the Great Tribulation, which will give us more of a guideline as to when the Mid-Tribulation Rapture event and the Post-Tribulation Rapture event may occur.

Now in the book of Daniel 12:12 it tells us whoever "waits and comes to the one thousand three hundred and thirty-five days" is blessed. We see it does not tell us why that person is blessed, only if he arrives to that point he will be blessed. Let us see if through exegesis and discernment we can determine what the why is. First, the Scriptures we have placed on our timetable tell us the sacrifice and offerings will cease sometime in the middle of the week and the abomination is set up at or around 1921 days. Because the Lord tells us all things are finished after 3½ years and the person who reaches the 1335th day is blessed we must take it to mean both periods end on the last day of the Tribulation Period. Therefore, we can add it to our timetable.

Nevertheless, there is an apparent discrepancy between the 3½ years, 1260 days and being blessed for reaching the 1335th day. Daniel 12:1, 7 tells us the Great Tribulation will be for a time, times and half a time, 1260 days, yet blessed is he that waits to the 1335th day. **Why is there a discrepancy of 75 days?** If you continue to read, this apparent discrepancy is explained in the final reconciliation. We must note if the "blessed person" promise ends at the coming of Jesus Christ/Yeshua HaMashiach, then that person would have to have been present at the beginning of the 1260th day, 3 ½ years, from the end of the Tribulation Period. This is in conjunction with the receiving of power by the anti-Christ/HaMashiach (the beast) for 42 months, 3½ years. I place this on the timetable because it is the survival of a Believer through the period of the rule of the anti-Christ/HaMashiach (beast) which causes the statement by the Lord, a person shall be blessed if he makes it to the 1335th day. Now let us place the 1335th day on our timetable. With this we now have all the times given in the Bible regarding the period of the Tribulation. Therefore, we can now look at all of the information we have placed on our timetable and decipher when the approximate times of the raptures shall occur so we can see it all works together for the good, that is, for The Tri-Tribulation Rapture. I will explain The Tri-Tribulation Rapture using the Biblical timetable and necessary additional scriptures.

Table VIII

Blessed is he who waits to the 1335th day

Daniel 12:12

Mid-point of the 70th Week

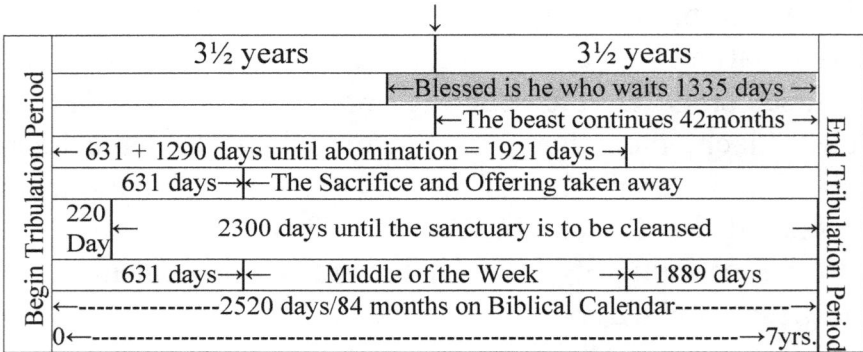

↓

Begin Tribulation Period	3½ years	3½ years	End Tribulation Period
		←Blessed is he who waits 1335 days →	
		←The beast continues 42months →	
	← 631 + 1290 days until abomination = 1921 days →		
	631 days→←The Sacrifice and Offering taken away		
	220 Day	← 2300 days until the sanctuary is to be cleansed →	
	631 days→← Middle of the Week →←1889 days		
	←---------------2520 days/84 months on Biblical Calendar-------------→		
	0←--→7yrs.		

Discerning the season for The Tri-Tribulation Rapture to occur

For those of us who are students of the Bible we have come to understand God has given through His chosen prophets, scribes, apostles and disciples certain types and shadows which foreshadow events to come. The type and shadows that will help us to discern when the raptures will occur are:

Matthew 24:37, 38 – Noah and the ark
Daniel 12:1b, 2 – a time of trouble for Israel

The above scriptures tell us, first, in the Lord Jesus Christ's/Yeshua HaMashiach's own words the people will be indulging in their own pleasures and giving no heed to the things of God and then the Son of Man shall come. How can we say this? Because God did not spare the antediluvian (before the flood) world with the exception of Noah and his family, 2 Peter 2:5. In Daniel 12:2, the Lord tells Daniel his people would undergo judgment and deliverance during the time of greatest trouble a nation has ever seen.

Romans 11:25 – until the fullness of the Gentiles

The fullness of the Gentiles refers to when God has determined the last of the Gentiles has been redeemed that shall be redeemed before the Tribulation Period and the time is right or has come for the Jews to be grafted back in. How does this fit in with when the rapture will occur? In each instance of the rapture it will not occur until the world of the unsaved will virtually be in total depravity; also, will not be completed until all of the Gentiles and Jews who are drawn by the Holy Spirit have received Jesus Christ/Yeshua HaMashiach as Lord, Savior, and God and have been redeemed. Finally, as Paul indicates, the Lord will take those whom the Lord will come for at His appearing for each event.

For the grace of God that brings salvation has appeared to all men, teaching us that, denying ungodliness and worldly lusts, we should live soberly, righteously, and godly in the present age, **looking for the blessed hope and glorious appearing of our great God and Savior Jesus Christ,** who gave Himself for us, that He might redeem us from every lawless deed and purify for Himself His own special people, zealous for good works. Titus 2:11-14 Emphasis added.

Therefore, we have type and shadow for all three of the events of The **Tri-Tribulation Rapture**: Pre-Tribulation – Noah entering the ark Matthew 24:37, 38; Mid-Tribulation – the fullness of the Gentiles, Romans 11:25; and Post-Tribulation – Jews shall be delivered, Daniel 12:1b, all Israel shall be saved, Romans 11:26, and redeem His special people Titus 2:14.

Who is the Church?

And He is the head of the body, the church, who is the beginning, the firstborn from the dead, that in all things He may have the preeminence. Colossians 1:18

Therefore, scripture says the Church is Christ/HaMashiach's body. Therefore, His body is made up of all who have believed in and received Jesus Christ/Yeshua HaMashiach as Lord, Savior, and God, Romans 12:5, Ephesians 4:15, 16. This includes Gentiles and Jews/Israelites. Now we must hold fast to the fact scripture makes no difference between Gentiles and Jews.

> For the Scripture says, "Whoever believes on Him will not be put to shame." For there is no distinction between Jew and Greek for the same Lord over all is rich to all who call upon Him. For whoever calls on the name of the Lord shall be saved. Romans 10:11-13

If then, there is no distinction between Jewish and Greek Believers, then saved Jews are members of the Body of Christ/HaMashiach, the Church. **Therefore, if saved, believing messianic Jews are members of the Church, the Church cannot replace Israel, for Israel is in part, the Church. On the other hand, unsaved Jews, Israelites, are no different from unsaved Gentiles who are not a part of the Church,** Romans chapter 11. With this, the argument for replacement theology is superfluous. Further, there is nowhere in the Bible it is said Israel is replaced. The fact is God says in the Bible He is married to Israel, Isaiah 54:4-8

If you would like more information about God being married to Israel, see Audrey L. Dickey, PhD's book, *God's Way and Marriage*, and on replacement Theology see Sid Roth's book, *The Incomplete Church*, chapter 4 (Roth 35).

What is notable is the beginning of the Church was almost entirely Jewish. Even today, God has not forgotten Israel, for there are many Jews in the Church, though most of Israel still rejects Christ/HaMashiach. However, we can say the same for the unsaved Gentiles and all the different religious cults, which at present outnumber the Church.

Therefore, we cannot be such an egotist as to think the Church has replaced the Jews, Israel, as God's people. Rather what we must seek to have in the Church as a whole is the *One New Man,* a union of Christian and Jewish Believers (Roth 130-31). Finally, be mindful of the fact in the entire 66 books of the Bible, the Old and New Testaments, which are for the Jews: the Torah, Tenakh, Ketuvim, and the B'rit Chadashah, there is only one Gentile writer and that is Luke. This should give us an inkling of how serious God is regarding the Jews and Israel. In fact, Jesus Christ/Yeshua HaMashiach gave the book of Revelation to a Jew, the Apostle John, on the Isle of Patmos. **What we know is, God is merciful, gracious and loving to even allow anyone Jew, Greek, or otherwise to come into His presence.** We cannot be so conceited as to think we **deserve** the slightest bit of God's mercy or grace; it was all His decision before the foundation of the world. For God knew the end before beginning, Isaiah 46:9, 10. That's why the book of Genesis 1:1 should be read as *'In beginning'* without the definite article to suggest there was a point in time that could be called *the* beginning, because it was His decision to begin and it was all finished when He began. Therefore, not knowing when He began to create we can only say, *in beginning* for God is eternal and exists outside of time and has no beginning or end.

In the book of Romans 11:11-36 the Apostle Paul tells us if God grafted in the Gentiles into the olive tree, the root of which is holy, and that tree became the church because of the work of Jesus Christ/HaMashiach then the church is, of course, Jews and Gentiles who believe. **If the**

Tribulation Period represents a last chance for unbelieving Israel to receive Jesus/Yeshua as Lord, Savior and God, then it also represents a last chance, in essence, for unbelieving Gentiles to receive Jesus/Yeshua as Lord, Savior and God as well. That is why today as we approach the Tribulation Period so many Jews are coming to the knowledge and belief Jesus/Yeshua is Messiah. However, there are the majority of Jews and Gentiles that do not receive Jesus Christ/Yeshua HaMashiach as Messiah. Here we have represented to us the olive tree as the church and the indication is God will graft the Jews in again. Therefore, those saved in the Tribulation Period are grafted into the olive tree (the Church).

Therefore, if the Church is the body of Christ/HaMashiach and the Church are people who have received Jesus/Yeshua as Lord, Savior and God, then those in the Tribulation Period who are in the Lord are in the body of Christ/HaMashiach and therefore in the *"Church."*

Pentecost (50 days after the resurrection of Jesus Christ/Yeshua HaMashiach), marked the official establishment of the Church with the Holy Spirit filling all who were in the Upper Room with His Spirit, Acts 2:1-4. Going further, we can deduce from the book of Daniel 9:25-26 Jerusalem would be rebuilt and Messiah, Jesus Christ/Yeshua HaMashiach, would be cut off, sacrificed, for the sin of the entire world by the 69th week. Therefore, we would have to say the Church Age began with the end of the 69th week with the death, burial and resurrection of the Lord Jesus Christ/Yeshua HaMashiach. It will certainly go on until the end of the 70th week, the Tribulation Period.

The Pre-Tribulation Rapture Event

I begin our reconciliation with the Pre-Tribulation Rapture event. The three events when taken together will complete God's plan for removing His people before assuming full reign over all nations and kingdoms of the earth.

By its very title the Pre-Tribulation Rapture event must occur before the Tribulation Period. The length of the Tribulation Period in my discussion in chapter 6 concerning the controversy as to when the event or events shall occur is seven years. Now, the key event, which will determine when the Tribulation Period shall begin, in the natural course of events as opposed to the Spiritual course of events, is the confirmation of the treaty Israel will make with its neighboring Arab countries. At least one author has said the treaty or covenant is about allowing Israel to perform sacrifice and offerings. This certainly could be a possibility for the scripture does say the prince will cause the sacrifice and offerings to end. Another possibility is the treaty is over land entitlement. As we know, the biggest contention is Israel's right to exist and/or possess land the Arab nations consider theirs.

Some discussion is appropriate as to how long before the Tribulation Period could it possibly occur.

> Let no one deceive you by any means; for that Day will not come unless the falling away comes first, and the man of sin is revealed, the son of perdition, 2 Thessalonians 2:3.

The son of perdition refers to the prince who is to come, Daniel 9:25, and is identified as the anti-Christ/HaMashiach, Daniel 7:25 and Revelation 13:2-5. Therefore, if The Pre-Tribulation Rapture cannot happen before the revealing of the son of perdition then the confirmation of the treaty will both reveal him and begin the seven-year Tribulation Period. Then events of the Tribulation Period must necessarily begin at the instant of the treaty signing. The possible exception to that theory is the signatories are revealed beforehand and therefore the rapture could happen sometime between the revealing of the signatories and the actual signing of the document. This we cannot know, which goes along with the scripture that says in Matthew 24:36, "But of that day and hour no one knows, not even the angels of heaven, but My Father only."

Probably the principal scripture that points to a Pre-Tribulation Rapture event is 1 Thessalonians 5:9: "For God did not appoint us to wrath, but to obtain salvation through our Lord Jesus Christ." This scripture points to the period of Great Tribulation Jesus/Yeshua speaks of in Matthew 24:15-21. Now referring back to the above-quoted scripture, it says we, those who have received Jesus Christ/Yeshua HaMashiach as Lord and Savior, "shall not" be appointed to the wrath of "The Day of the Lord." Verse six of the passage tells us to be sober and watchful. Verse 10 tells us whether we are asleep or awake when the Lord comes we will live with Him.

While the above is the most direct scripture passage stating we will not go through the Tribulation Period there are others.

For they themselves declare concerning us what manner of entry we had to you, and how you turned to God from idols to serve the living and true God, and to wait for his Son from heaven, whom He raised from the dead, even Jesus who delivers us from the wrath to come. 1 Thessalonians 1:9, 10

This is stating Jesus will come from heaven to deliver us from the wrath to come. The definite article, *the,* speaks of a specific time of wrath, which chapter 5 of 1 Thessalonians explains, is the wrath of the "Day of the Lord", the Tribulation Period.

Another verifying scripture that those in Christ will not experience the wrath of God is in the book of Revelation:

Because you have kept My command to persevere, I also will keep you from the hour of trial which shall come upon the whole world, to test those who dwell on the earth. Revelation 3:10

This scripture is concerning Jesus Christ/Yeshua HaMashiach speaking to one of the seven churches in Asia in the book of Revelation chapters 2 and 3. We know this is speaking to our generation because to the present there has not been a trial that has come upon the entire earth. Another of the seven churches He did not have anything against, will have to endure some tribulation before they receive their reward. Therefore, because we know the Tribulation is forthcoming and still before us, this scripture is a comfort knowing we will not experience this trial, which is to come upon the whole earth. What we must also understand is He is also speaking to five other churches, which have other characteristics to which He did not make this promise. What is my point? Well, the promise is not to every 'church type' to go in the Pre-Tribulation Rapture event just because they are a church *'labeled'* Christian. This statement was to *'this'* church, which He had nothing against because it is the *'faithful'* church, called the church in Philadelphia, the other church is the church in Smyrna, "The Persecuted Church." These are the only churches our Lord Jesus Christ/Yeshua HaMashiach does not have anything against them. The strongest thing He has to say to the church in Philadelphia is "Hold fast to what you have, that no one may take your crown," Revelation 3:11. Then to the church in Smyrna, "Be faithful until death," if necessary, Revelation 2:10. What can we draw from this? Jesus speaks to the churches in: Ephesus, Pergamos, Thyatira, Sardis, and Laodicea. He tells them they must overcome in order to meet Him in the Pre-Tribulation Rapture. While this is a strong statement and seemingly harsh and judgmental, I would ask that chapters 2 and 3 of the book of Revelation be read in order to come to your own conclusion. **Of course, there are exceptions in each of the foregoing church types because there are faithful Believers in most if not all church types. The faithful Believers, of course, will go in the catching away. This in itself will be a sign to those who find themselves left after the rapture event that they will need to repent and be faithful in order to**

go in the next event. According to my reconciliation, you will have almost seven years to be a part of one of the two remaining rapture events. As harsh as this may seem, there is a blessing because our Lord and Savior is merciful and full of grace in that there is a space of time for anyone who may find themselves on the earth after the Pre-Tribulation Rapture event to repent and be faithful to the Lord Jesus Christ/Yeshua HaMashiach.

The fourth passage speaking to the Pre-Tribulation Rapture is:

> Now, brethren, concerning the coming of our Lord Jesus Christ and our gathering together to Him, we ask you, not to be soon shaken in mind or troubled, either by spirit or by word or by letter, as if from us, as though the day of Christ had come. Let no one deceive you by any means; for that Day will not come unless the falling away comes first, and the man of sin is revealed, the son of perdition, 2 Thessalonians 2:1-3

Paul, here, tells the Thessalonians three things:

1. Not to be worried or troubled because the Day of Christ had not come.
2. The Day would not come without Believers falling away from the faith first.
3. The revealing of the man of sin (the anti-Christ) is after the falling away.

For us, we know we must be close because there are so many that have fallen away from the faith. Therefore, the revealing of the anti-Christ is the final piece. However, we may likely not know when the revealing is because the one who is the anti-Christ will probably be determined when he confirms the treaty. Signing the treaty, by definition, the rapture of Pre-Tribulation Saints/Believers will happen in a twinkling of an eye.

> Behold, I tell you a mystery: We shall not all sleep, but we shall all be changed – **in a moment, in the twinkling of an eye,** at the last trumpet. For the trumpet will sound and the dead will be raised incorruptible and we shall be changed. 1 Corinthians 15:51-52 Emphasis added.

Many Pre-Tribulation proponents believe the book of Revelation 5:11 speaks of a 100 plus millions of angels, elders and possibly Believers around the throne of God worshipping the Lamb of God, Jesus/Yeshua, and it supports the Pre-Tribulation Rapture event. In verse 13, it does say every creature in heaven, which would include all Believers who are redeemed, say the blessing over God the Father and the Lamb of God. However, at this point we cannot say this would include any raptured Believers because of the unopened seals. **If seals one through five have yet to be opened then it is unlikely these are Pre-Tribulation Raptured Believers because seals one through five encompass the entire church age from the time the revelation is given to John.** What Revelation 4 and 5 are giving us is a picture of the throne of God and all that is in the immediate vicinity of the throne. Heaven is vast and beyond our imaginations. Besides, think of a natural situation of a play or concert or any large public event. The action of what is taking place is in a small area or arena in comparison to the crowds surrounding it. Well, what we are visualizing in chapters 4 and 5 is the stage area and not the entire body of Christ that must be surrounding the stage. Then too, we must allow for the omni-dimensional aspect of God and the above is an ongoing sequence throughout the Tribulation Period. It is possible with our three-dimensional concept we just cannot grasp and put the rapture in its proper context.

Finally, the question as to the exact timing of the Pre-Tribulation Rapture event is not calculable because there is no actual statement in scripture in relation to when it shall occur in time. The only event we can relate it to is the confirming of the peace treaty between Israel and the Arab nations. Therefore, we know in order to be Pre-Tribulation it would have to happen in at least a "twinkling of an eye" before the signing of the treaty is completed. On the other hand, it could have to do with when the wrath of God began which is in the book of Revelation 6:12 and the opening of the sixth seal. We know the opening of the sixth seal begins the wrath of God because it says in the 17th verse, "For the great day of His wrath has come, and who is able to stand." Inasmuch as there are no time factors given for the beginning of the wrath of God, we cannot say when the wrath of God will start. Will it be gradual? Will it be sudden with the earthquake in verse 12 and coincide with the signing of the treaty? This we do not know. The Lord uses the example of Noah and the ark to say they did not know until the flood came and then it was too late for salvation from the flood. However, Noah, a righteous man and his family, were safely secured within the ark when the flood came. The same holds true with the rapture events, if you do not have salvation at the time of the event, you will not have time for salvation for the event happens in a twinkling of an eye.

There are things scripture says that can give us an inkling we are very near to the 70th week of Daniel 9:27. Jesus/Yeshua said:

> Now learn this parable from the fig tree: When its branch has already become tender and puts forth leaves, you know that summer is near. So, you also, when you see all these things, know that it is near – at the doors! Assuredly, I say to you, this generation will by no means pass away till all these things take place. Heaven and earth will pass away, but My words will by no means pass away. Matthew 24:32-33

The key words are "this generation will by no means pass away until all these things take place." So, the question is what are "all these things"? These things would be all Jesus/Yeshua said pertaining to the question the disciples asked regarding the end of the age. Let us enumerate His answers:

1. False Christs
2. Wars and rumors of wars

3. Nations rise against nations, kingdom against kingdom
4. Famines, pestilences, and earthquakes
5. Tribulation
6. Be killed
7. Hated by all nations for My name's sake
8. Betray and hate one another
9. False prophets
10. Lawlessness will abound
11. Love will grow cold
12. Then He says the one who endures to the end of all these things shall be saved

He was not speaking of just soul salvation, but salvation of the soul *and* taken in a rapture event. These are the *things* found in Matthew 24:5-14. Jesus/Yeshua then turns His attention to what happens during the 70th week of Daniel 9:27. He refers to it as great tribulation, which the world has not experienced, Matthew 24:15-25. Then Jesus/Yeshua gives account of His Second Coming, Matthew 24:26-31.

In addition to the above in the Biblical year of 5775, we were in the midst of a Blood Moon Tetrad, which fulfills Joel 2:30-31, Mark 13:24 in which the Sun turns to darkness and moon turns to blood. This happens before the Tribulation Period begins. Not only the sun and the moon change but also, they change on Biblically appointed days: First of Nissan, the Biblical New Year; the 15th of Nisan, Passover (Pesach); and the 15th of Tishrei, Tabernacles (Sukkot). Another indicator is the year, 5775 was a year of release, a Shemittah year, Biblically. In addition, following this Shemittah year was a Jubilee year. For all these significant events to occur at the same time could enter into "all these things" Jesus/Yeshua was referring to. Historically Blood moons, Shemittah years and Jubilee years have signaled major events in Israel's history. **Now for all to converge together in the same year and in a month of God's appointed Feasts could point to an awesome event about to occur**. Which could be the signing of the covenant of Daniel 9:27 with its concurrent rapture of the Church. Because God does His greatest events according to His appointed feasts/mo'adim, we should be all the more watchful during the appointed feasts/mo'adim. The Lord was crucified on Passover/Pesach and He rose on the first day of the Feast of Unleavened Bread; the Church began at Pentecost/Shavuot; the Blood Moons occurred on Passover and Sukkot/Feast of Tabernacles, so why would the Pre-Tribulation Rapture not occur on the Feast of Yom Teruah/Feast of Trumpets.

However, understand if you miss the catching away in the first rapture event, according to scripture you will have opportunity to be raptured in a subsequent rapture. Because we do not know the day nor the hour, it is a must that you make your salvation sure by receiving the Lord Jesus Christ/Yeshua HaMashiach as your Lord and Savior now. To do that go to the salvation prayer page, repeat the prayer and believe it with your heart and God will save you. Yes! It is that simple. The key is to say it with your mouth and believe it in your heart; I praise the Lord for your salvation!

If the Pre-Tribulation Rapture Catching Away occurs the instant before the signing of the treaty, then the length of the Tribulation Period is 2520 days from that point. If you miss it, remember you have two more chances, but living will become much more difficult, it would be much better to go up on the first trip and enjoy being in the presence of the Lord!

The Mid-Tribulation Rapture Event

After having established the biblical evidence for the Pre-Tribulation Rapture Event, one might say there are many scriptures found in the Holy Bible, which support a rapture event other than a Pre-Tribulation event. Well, that is exactly my point and is why one has to conclude there is more than one event. **Therefore, if we can show well-founded scriptures that support an event other than the Pre-Tribulation event then we only need to place them in the category of whether the event is mid-tribulational or post-tribulational.**

I have established that Revelation 6:12 gives us the beginning of God's wrath. Therefore, any scriptures that are indicating a rapture event from here until Revelation 19:11 would tell us there are more than one rapture event. You might say I am building a catch 22 because I have said God starts, stops, and repeats in order to get His point across and might this not be that same scenario. **The point is well taken, except we are dealing with whether something has happened prior to or during this period, defined as the Tribulation Period.** What I am saying is after the beginning if anything happens between the beginning and the end it has to point to something other than that which happened before the beginning whether or not the information is circuitous (twisty) or not.

Revelation 7 begins with, "after these things," which indicates all of Revelation 6 has already occurred.

> After these things I looked and behold, a great multitude which no one could number, of all nations, tribes, peoples, and tongues, standing before the throne and before the Lamb, clothed with white robes, with palm branches in their hands. Revelation 7:9

Revelation 7:9-16 tell us Believers came out of the Great Tribulation, not before the Great Tribulation. Therefore, how did they get there except by death or by a rapture? I make this point now, if these are present and have come out of the Great Tribulation and the Apostle Paul says the dead shall rise first and those who are alive shall join them then these from the Great Tribulation, whether by death or alive, must have arrived by a rapture. Then this scripture supports a Mid-Tribulation Rapture. I make note this occurs after Jesus Christ/Yeshua HaMashiach opens the sixth seal. The multitude we saw before the throne in chapter 5 verse eight are Believers redeemed by the Lamb before the Great Tribulation. In addition, the souls of those martyred for the sake of Jesus Christ/Yeshua HaMashiach are under the altar in the throne of God, Revelation 6:9. All are already in the *throne room* before the Lamb opens the sixth seal.

> Then one of the elders answered, saying to me, "Who are these arrayed in white robes, and where did they come from?" And I said to him, "Sir, you know." So he said to me, "These are the ones who come out of the great tribulation, and washed their robes and made them white in the blood of the Lamb. Revelation 7:13-14

What we have here are statements in the throne room before God, a great multitude of people out **of all nations who have come out of the Great Tribulation**. Therefore, having come out of the Great Tribulation and the seventh seal has not as yet been opened tells us Jesus/Yeshua considers the entire period of seven years to be the Great Tribulation Period and the Mid-Tribulation Rapture has occurred. However, for our purposes, **because the greatest period of the greatest wrath of God begins after the opening of the seventh seal in Revelation 8:1, I designate verse five, as most do, the beginning of The Great Tribulation Period.**

Now, I would like to point out the action of the angel throwing the censer filled with fire to the earth signals the beginning of the Great Tribulation. Therefore, we have this exegesis of what is going on between Revelation 6:17 and 8:5. I would have to say God is giving pause to tell us the Mid-Tribulation Rapture is happening at this point. Therefore, I would say the event happens just prior to the beginning of the Great Tribulation Period and the opening of the seventh seal.

Further proof of there being Believers during the Tribulation Period is found in Revelation 12:15, which in essence, says the nations Satan controls come against Israel with their best effort and strength. Nevertheless, cannot prevail because there are enough nations of the world that will protect Israel, verse 16, and absorb the hit of the nations that are against Israel by swallowing the flood. Finally, the dragon turns from the Jews, Israel, to the Believers, Revelation 12:17. These are Believers because it says those "who keep the commandments of God and have the testimony of Jesus Christ." We understand these are those saved during the Tribulation Period while Israel is protected for 3½ years, probably the first 3½ years. I say the first 3½ years because Daniel 12:7 says:

> "that it shall be for a time, times, and half a time; and when the power of the holy people has been completely shattered, all these things shall be finished."

If all things shall be finished after the holy people, Israel and Believers, have their power shattered then they would certainly have to be in a period of time when they are not protected. Therefore, the power of the Believers would have to be shattered in the last 3½ years, Revelation 13:5-7. The protection of Israel is during the first 3½ years of the Tribulation Period.

Now Islam, that is, those who are Islamic fundamentalists, especially the Shi'ite Muslims, who want to annihilate Israel from the earth, begin to attack the new remnant of Christians, and Jewish Messianic Believers in the world especially in the Middle East, Revelation 12:17.

This proves there are Believers present in the first 3½ years of the Tribulation Period. In addition, this tells us Believers are present just prior to the consolidation of the power of the anti-Christ/HaMashiach.

At this point, let me give an exegesis according to my timetable. In the table below, I have placed the scripture references for times that affect the possible occurrence of the rapture event, in this case the Mid-Tribulation Rapture event. From the table I will explain the possible period in which the event may take place.

Table IX-a

The Mid-Tribulation Rapture Event

Mid-point of the 70th Week

Begin Tribulation Period	First 3 ½ years	Second 3 ½ years	End Tribulation Period
		Blessed is he who waits 1335 days →	
		← The Beast continues 42 months→	
	←631 + 1290 days until Abomination = 1921 days →		
	631 days→|←The Sacrifice and Offering taken away		
	220 Day | ←	2300 days until the sanctuary is to be cleansed →	
	631 days→|← Middle of the Week →|←1889 days		
	---------- 2520 days/84 months on Biblical Calendar----------→		
	0←------------------------------------→7yrs		

Israel rebuilds the Temple and re-institutes sacrifices and offerings. The rebuilt Temple most likely occurs before the signing of treaty with Israel's neighboring Islamic countries. We can assume the Temple is already in place because of no mention of the completion is in the book of Daniel chapter 9 and is only mentioned in

Revelation 11:1-3 to say the Temple is there and Gentiles trample down its outer court for 42 months.

Therefore, the Temple does exist during the Tribulation Period. Daniel 9:27 says the prince shall put an end to Israel's sacrifices and offerings in the middle of the week. Therefore, the Temple has to at least be completed sometime in the middle of the week for the sacrifices and offerings to be ended therein. Daniel 8:14 tells us the Temple will be cleansed after 2300 days, so the Temple survives until the end. The anti-Christ receives authority to continue for 42 months according to the book of Revelation 13:5. The end of the 42 months given anti-Christ/HaMashiach to continue must be the end of his reign and the Tribulation Period, for scripture says:

> Then the beast was captured, and with him the false prophet who worked signs in his presence, by which he deceived those who received the mark of the beast and those who worshiped his image. These two were cast alive into the lake of fire burning with brimstone. Revelation 19:20

Then we know the 42 months ends at or before the coming of the Lord Jesus Christ/Yeshua HaMashiach who will cleanse the sanctuary.

Daniel 12:11 says the abomination of desolation is set-up 1290 days after the sacrifice and offering has ended. Let us digest what we have so far. The prince puts an end to sacrifice and offerings in the middle of the week. This tells us the end of sacrifice and offerings must occur at or after the 631st day and before the 1889th day. The vision of sacrifice and offerings covers 2300 days at the end of which the cleansing of the sanctuary occurs and will be at the end of the Tribulation period. A possible importance of the 2300 days is to indicate the time that the Tribulation Temple is finished and ready to begin sacrifice and offerings. A period, which begins before the middle of the week, 220 days after the confirmation of the treaty and includes the 631st day of the Tribulation Period, which would be the earliest possible day of the middle of the week. Therefore, for simplicity sake, I will establish the end of sacrifice and offering occurs at the 631st day. In addition, I designate this is also the earliest date the Mid-Tribulation Rapture can occur.

Now to establish the latest time the event can take place we look at the prince of Daniel 9:27. First, let us establish where we are. I said the Mid-Tribulation Rapture happens before Revelation chapter 8, which is before the Great Tribulation. In addition, Satan does not turn his attention to the Believers in earnest until the second 3½-year period, which is the Great Tribulation. What we have is a period in the first 3½ years in which the world will be recovering physically and emotionally from the first rapture event. At the same time, Satan will be trying to destroy Israel, Revelation 12:13-14, whereas the "two wings of a great eagle," which many take to mean the eagle represents the United States, protects Israel. Following through to Revelation 13:5, the authority given the beast (anti-Christ/HaMashiach) is to continue for 42 months. That authority has to end at the end of the Tribulation Period because of his capture in Revelation

19:20, which occurs at the battle of Armageddon, Revelation 16:16. Therefore, his grant of authority I take as complete world rulership and must begin at or about the exact middle of the Tribulation Period. In order for the rapture event to happen before the giving of authority to the anti-Christ/HaMashiach it would have to happen on or before the last instant before giving the authority to the beast (anti-Christ/HaMashiach). Hence, the rapture event must take place prior to the full furor of the anti-Christ/HaMashiach, which will be at the halfway point (1260 days) and the beginning of the Great Tribulation Period, Revelation 8:5.

Finally, there is one more piece of information I believe will affect the rapture events and that is Daniel 12:12 in which the Lord says, **"Blessed is he who waits, and comes to the one thousand three hundred and thirty-five days."** How do I explain this period the Lord has given us? **The implication (suggestion) is to make it until the return of the Lord at His Second Advent to put down all rebellion**. We arrive at this because the end of the 1335 days would necessarily be at the time Jesus/Christ Yeshua/HaMashiach returns at His Second Advent. Therefore, if we subtract the 1335 days from the seven years, we end up with the 1185th day. Well if we look at Matthew 24:22, the Lord says, "And unless those days were shortened, no flesh would be saved; but for the elect's sake those days will be shortened." Because He, the Lord, has shortened the time to endure and the fact He has said the survivor of the 1335 days is blessed informs us from that point until the end or near the end of the Tribulation Period there will not be a rapture event. Obviously, we must conclude the Mid-Tribulation event must occur at or prior to the 1335th day before the end of the Tribulation Period.

The time narrowed down for the Mid-Tribulation Rapture event to happen is between the 631st day and the 1185th day after the treaty confirmation, a period of 554 days or 18½ months.

Table IX-b

The Mid-Tribulation Rapture Event Reconciled

Mid-point of the 70th Week

	First 3 ½ years		Second 3 ½ years	
Begin Tribulation Period	631 days→ 1185th day>		Blessed is he who waits 1335 days →	End Tribulation Period
	631 days→ 1185th day>	75 days	←The Beast continues 42 months→	
	← 631 + 1290 days until abomination =1921 days →			
	631 days→ ←The Sacrifice and Offering taken away			
220 days	← 2300 days until the sanctuary is to be cleansed →			
	631 days→← Middle of the Week →←1889 days			
	←----------------2520 days/84 months on Biblical Calendar----------------→			
0←--→7yrs				

According to the table above, it would be my choice, the Mid-Tribulation event would be on the 1185th day or very close and before that. Because It would fulfill the prophecies of Mathew 24:22 and Jesus Christ/Yeshua HaMashiach saying the days would be shortened for the elect's sake. Also, it explains the Daniel 12:12 passage on waiting the 1335 days to be blessed. On the other hand, to put it another way, it shall happen '75' days before the beast receives power to continue for 42 months.

The Post-Tribulation Rapture Event

Our final event, the Post-Tribulation Rapture event, I will begin with the scripture that most justifies both the Mid-Tribulation and Post-Tribulation events, Hebrews 13:8: "Jesus Christ is the same yesterday, today, and forever." Therefore, because the Lord Jesus Christ/Yeshua HaMashiach is the same yesterday, today, and forever and is not a respecter of persons, Romans 2:11, He will not just take some of *His* people who become *The Believers* (Saints) in any portion of the Tribulation Period. They will *ALL* be raptured. Because of the Pre-Tribulation Believers catching away, it signifies **the tribulation Believers in both the Mid-Tribulation and Post-Tribulation Rapture events are caught away also**. We understand from scripture there will be Believers who will have to give their lives in martyrdom (Revelation 14:13). These will become, along with they who die of natural causes, those who died in Christ and will rise first in the Rapture. However, those who survive to the appointed times of the rapture events will be caught up and meet the Lord in the clouds of the air (1 Thessalonians 4:16-17). This signals there will be a length of time for those who are still here, *'after'* the Mid-Tribulation Rapture event, to receive Jesus Christ/Yeshua HaMashiach, as Lord and Savior. After which they will participate in the last of the rapture events.

Before we go further into the evidence for a Post-Tribulation Rapture, I want to establish that events in

Revelation are now occurring chronologically with periodic scriptural explanation of events layered on top of other events. First, the language used tells us *"after this"* or *"after these things"* indicates an event occurs following another event. Also, starting with Revelation 6:1 Jesus/Yeshua begins to open the seals of the scroll, which chronicles the events prior to the beginning of the Tribulation Period. Thereafter events occur in chronological order in the Tribulation period. Now chapter 7 begins with *"After these things ..."* which indicates that which has happened is past and we are going on to future events.

I would like to point out again the action of the angel throwing the censer, which has the prayers of the Believers, to the earth signals the beginning of the Great Tribulation (Revelation 8:5). Therefore, the events leading up to the Great Tribulation begin with the opening of the seventh seal in Revelation 8:1. The seven angels sound seven trumpets, which will be the order of the events for the Great Tribulation, which are the final judgments of God on the earth. The Great Tribulation climaxes at the gathering of the nations at Armageddon, Hebrew for Hill at Megiddo (Revelation 16:16). In Revelation 16:17 it says, *"It is done!"*

Looking at the Great Tribulation, the last half or the final 1260 days of the rule of the anti-Christ, we find many non-Believers have become Believers. They are still on earth and have become the Kingdom of God on earth. These will be mostly Jews and perhaps a few non-Jewish Believers who finally come into the knowledge and belief in Jesus/Yeshua as Lord, Savior and God. Hence, there has to be a point at which these Believers are raptured in order to participate in the Marriage Supper of the Lamb (Revelation 19:7-9). There is no alluding to in scripture of Believers being raptured/caught up and immediately returning with Christ/HaMashiach.

When will The Post-Tribulation Rapture occur?

The Post-Tribulation Rapture will occur within the last 75 days of the Tribulation Period. Many may think this is a contradiction or error but it is neither for it provides a way for the Post-Tribulation Raptured Saints/Believers to attend the Marriage Supper of the Lamb to receive their rewards.

> The nations were angry and your wrath has come, and the time of the dead, that they should be judged, and that you should reward your servants the prophets and the saints, and those who fear your name, small and great, and should destroy those who destroy the earth. Revelation 11:18

The above scripture confirms the rewards of all Saints/Believers. 1 Corinthians 3:13 tells us **"the Day"** will declare what sort of reward we shall receive. The Apostle is telling us when we get to the Day of the Lord, which will be during the seven-year Tribulation Period, our *rewards* will be determined. The scripture quoted above is in chapter 11, which is after the sixth trumpet of the seventh seal and after the second woe has finished.

What has transpired to this point of Revelation 11:18, is in Revelation 9:1-12 the fifth trumpet of the seventh seal sounds and the first of three woes begins. Chapter 11 verses 1 and 2 are regarding the Temple of God and the fact Gentiles (non-Believers probably Muslim) shall trample the outer court for 42 months, 3½ years. The ministry of the two witnesses follows in the third verse and is for 1260 days, 3½ years. The beginning of their 3½ years I place at the Mid-Tribulation Rapture in order that their ministry will end with the beginning of the 75 days before the end of the Tribulation Period to coincide with the Post-Tribulation Rapture. Chapter 11 makes the point the beast kills the two witnesses at the end of their ministry, but they resurrect after 3½ days. These are probably a literal 3½ days because their bodies remain on display and not put in graves. After resurrecting and being summoned to ascend into heaven bodily, their enemies witness their ascension. This marks the end of the second woe (Revelation 11:14).

The last woe, which is the seventh trumpet, has begun and heaven announces its claim *"the kingdoms of this world have become the kingdoms of our Lord and of His Christ"* (Revelation 11:15). Because it comes after the rapture of two of the three rapture events, Revelation 11:18 confirms all Believers will be at the Marriage Supper of the Lamb. You might say this is too far in advance to be speaking of the Post-Tribulation event. Well, it is much closer to the end than to the mid-point of the period. In addition, it is after the sounding of the seventh trumpet of the seventh seal.

Jesus tells us in the book of Matthew:

> And unless those days were shortened, no flesh would be saved; but for the elect's sake those days will be shortened. Matthew 24:22

We can surmise the elect (Believers) will not have to go through the entire tribulation of "those days." The elect of "those days" would be referring to the Jews and Gentiles that have missed the Mid-Tribulation Rapture. They now have become born again. Therefore, they must go through the Great Tribulation. The shortening of "those days" refer to the 75 days before the end of the tribulation period when the Post-Tribulation Rapture event occurs. The 75-day shortening period is also reflected in the Mid-Tribulation Rapture event. The 1185th day is 75 days shorter than the mid-point of the seven-year tribulation period. In Matthew 24:29, 30 the Lord speaks of His Second Coming "after" the tribulation of "those days." **This tells us what happens to the elect in the Tribulation Period is entirely separate from His Second Coming.**

Now the scripture that points to the Post-Tribulation event is, first of all, Revelation 13:7 that grants authority to the anti-Christ to make war with the Saints/Believers. This tells us there are Saints/Believers present during this period after giving the anti-Christ/HaMashiach authority to continue for 42 months. He in fact makes war with them and overcomes them. We know he does not overcome all because Daniel 12:12 proclaims a blessing over those who make it to the 1335th day which would encompass the entire period of the anti-Christ's being granted authority.

In addition, Revelation 14:13 tells us there are Believers in heaven who did not take the mark of the beast. Therefore, we need to build a solid foundation based on scripture for the Post-Tribulation Rapture event. Probably the most definitive scriptures are those in Revelation saying:

> Then I looked, and behold, a white cloud, and on the cloud sat One like the Son of Man, having on His head a golden crown, and in His hand a sharp sickle. And another angel came out of the temple, crying with a loud voice to Him who sat on the cloud, "Thrust in Your sickle and reap, for the time has come for You to reap, for the harvest of the earth is ripe." So, He who sat on the cloud thrust in His sickle on the earth, and the earth was reaped. Revelation 14:14-16

Here the angel is speaking to Jesus Christ/Yeshua HaMashiach Himself who is in the clouds of the air, which speaks itself of the rapture. The angel tells the Son of Man to thrust in His sickle and reap the harvest of Believers on the earth. We know this is Jesus/Yeshua because it refers to Him as the Son of Man. The Bible translators in every recognized translation refer here to Him and begin Him in the upper case, which honors His deity. Because of the scripture's location in the book of Revelation we know they are referring to the Post-Tribulation Rapture event because it comes totally after chapter 13 and the scripture of Revelation 14:13 which itself explains the success of the Believers who do not take the mark of the *beast.*

Table X

The Post-Tribulation Rapture Event Reconciled

Mid-point of the 70th Week

Mid-point of the 70th Week

	First 3 ½ years		Second 3 ½ years	
Begin Tribulation Period	631 days→ 1185th day→		Blessed is he who waits 1335 days →	End Tribulation Period
	The Mid-Tribulation R/CA→	75 days	← The rule of the Beast Post-Tribulation Rapture →	75 Days
	631 days→ 1185th day→	75 days	← The Beast continues 42months →	
	← 631 + 1290 days until abomination = 1921 days →			
	631 days→←The Sacrifice and Offering taken away			
	220 Days ← 2300 days until the sanctuary is to be cleansed →			
	631 days→← Middle of the Week →←1889 days			
	←--------------2520 days/84 months on Biblical Calendar------------------→			
	0←--→7yrs.			

To further confirm this, the rest of the harvest is thrown into "the great winepress of the wrath of God" (Revelation 14:19). As though this were not enough, Revelation 15:2 tells us John sees the Believers, who did not receive the mark, in heaven standing on a sea of glass. John then sees *"after these things"* the angels with the seven last plagues are preparing to act. If then we have the Believers, who are victorious over not receiving the mark of the beast, here on the sea of glass, then the Post-Tribulation Rapture is completed. Then Revelation 14:16 has to be the rapture.

All these things occur before the final wrath of God. We may then surmise all of the rapture events occur before the Marriage Supper of the Lamb is ended (Revelation 19:9). Therefore, we can say all Believers are on board and in heaven attending the Marriage Supper of the Lamb.

I will now give the exegesis, as far as the Post-Tribulation Rapture event is concerned, from the timetable.

The Marriage Supper of the Lamb

We must understand the Lord will shorten the days for the Believers in the second half of the Tribulation Period as He did for the Believers in the first half of the Tribulation Period. Therefore, the Lord will shorten by 75 days the period between the Rule of the anti-Christ and the return of the Lord to rule and reign. This is not a discrepancy but a time intentionally placed to allow the Post-Tribulation Rapture event to occur and give time for these Believers to participate in the Marriage Supper of the Lamb. This is because the Marriage Supper of the Lamb is the proper time to bless **all** Believers. It includes the giving of rewards to the Believers who have crowns and good works in Jesus Christ/Yeshua HaMashiach that merit recognition:

> For no other foundation can anyone lay than that which is laid, which is Jesus Christ. Now if anyone builds on this foundation with gold, silver, precious stones, wood, hay, straw, each one's work will become clear; for **the Day** will declare it, because it will be revealed by

fire; and the fire will test each one's work, of what sort it is. If any one's work which he has built on it endures, he will receive a reward. If anyone's work is burned, he will suffer loss; but he himself will be saved, yet so as through fire. 1 Corinthians 3:11-15 Emphasis added.

This passage tells us rewards will be given to Believers who do works that will build on the foundation of Jesus Christ/Yeshua HaMashiach. These rewards will be given during **"the Day"** of the Lord. **The Day of the Lord is the Tribulation Period.** Why do I say this? Well Revelation 6:17 says, "For the great day of His wrath has come." I believe this statement refers to the entire 3½ years verses 12-17 cover. We know the wrath of the Lamb, verse 16, is the wrath of God and the Day of the Lord is a metaphor for the wrath of God. Therefore, all of the wrath of God poured out from Revelation chapter 8 thru 16 must be a part of the Day of the Lord. So, the Day of the Lord is seven years, then I believe the Marriage Supper of the Lamb is seven years also. Therefore, the rewards to Believers/Saints given in heaven is at the Marriage Supper of the Lamb during the seven-year duration of the Marriage Supper. Understand, *rewards* involve Old Testament Believers/Saints as well as New Testament. Therefore, the Marriage Supper serves all of the billions of Believers since Adam. In order to complete and do justice to all Believers/Saints the seven years of the Tribulation Period will be needed. That is why we have the 75-day period during the time of the anti-Christ and the

Lord's return, so those of the Post-Tribulation Rapture may receive their rewards before returning with the Lord to rule and reign on the earth.

Now, let us turn to our timetable in order to determine and explain according to the scriptures the Post-Tribulation Rapture event. First of all, the scripture that brings it all together for the Post-Tribulation event is Daniel 12:12. I believe the Lord is saying the Believers who have missed the first two rapture events and have made it through all the anti-Christ/HaMashiach (the beast) has dished out and reached the Marriage Supper of the Lamb have to be blessed people. The majority of these Saints/Believers will be Jews. What is significant about this period is the counting of the days begin from the point of the Mid-Tribulation Rapture event. From that point, the anti-Christ/HaMashiach will give a high priority to destroying all Saints/Believers.

> It was granted to him to make war with the saints and to overcome them. And authority was given him over every tribe, tongue, and nation. Revelation 13:7

From this, we gather the anti-Christ is on a search and destroy mission against those who have come to Christ/HaMashiach since the Mid-Tribulation Rapture event. In addition, the anti-Christ/HaMashiach appoints a second anti-Christ/HaMashiach, a religious false prophet, to cause the whole world to worship the first anti-Christ/HaMashiach. Not only that, he causes the whole world to receive the mark of the beast, the anti-

Christ/HaMashiach (Revelation 13:16). I point these scriptures out because through all of this the majority of the Jews have not relinquished their position that Jesus Christ is not their Messiah. However, when the abomination of desolation is set up in the holy place, which occurs at 1921 days after the signing of the treaty, the anti-Christ/HaMashiach (the son of perdition) is the one:

> Who opposes and exalts himself above all that is called God or that is worshiped, so that he sits as God in the temple of God, showing himself that he is God. 2 Thessalonians 2:4

How do I arrive at 1921 days? Daniel 12:11 tells us "the abomination" occurs 1290 days after sacrifice and offerings are taken away. The sacrifice and offerings taken away in the middle of the week at the 631st day is the earliest point that can be the middle of the week. If we add 1290 to that, we arrive at the 1921st day as the earliest point for "the abomination" to occur. The latest it could occur would be 2449th day and still allow the Post-Tribulation Rapture to occur. I choose the earlier date because the Lord says in Matthew 24:15-25 to flee for then will be the greatest tribulation ever known. I take this to mean there has to be time for those left:

1. To flee the anti-Christ/HaMashiach's all-out effort to destroy the Jews (Revelation 13:7)
2. To leave house and home (Matthew 24:16-20)

3. To experience the worst of the Great Tribulation (Matthew 24:21)
4. To have the days shortened for the elect's sake (Mathew 24:22)
5. To believe no one is Christ/HaMashiach, except the one that comes from heaven (Matthew 24:23-27)

Upon the display of the abomination of desolation the Orthodox, conservative and other religious Jews are going to rebel against the anti-Christ/HaMashiach. The abomination of desolation is the fact this man will declare himself God, 2 Thessalonians 2:4. This will be equal to declaring war. It is at this point the majority of Jews will turn against the anti-Christ/HaMashiach and declare Jesus/Yeshua is the true HaMashiach/Christ. The scriptural reference is Yeshua/Jesus telling the disciples:

> Therefore when you see the abomination of desolation, spoken of by Daniel the prophet standing in the holy place (whoever reads let him understand) then let those who are in Judea flee to the mountains. Matthew 24:15, 16

At this point Believers the anti-Christ/HaMashiach is trying to destroy are both Jewish and Christian Believers who have the testimony of Yeshua/Jesus because they, the Jews, will have received:

1. The testimony of the two witnesses God has sent to earth to prophesy for 1260 days, 3½ years (Revelation 11:3).

2. In addition, the 144,000 Israelites sealed, as servants of God are witnesses to all Israel during the rule of the anti-Christ/HaMashiach (Revelation 7:2-8).

3. Finally, in Revelation 14:6 there is an angel who preaches the everlasting gospel to those who dwell on the earth.

When will The Post-Tribulation Rapture occur? The Post-Tribulation Rapture will occur within the last 75 days. More specifically, it will happen at the killing of the two witnesses, or possibly, at or after their resurrection. You see, the ministry of the two witnesses begin at the Mid-Tribulation Rapture, that is, 75 days before the anti-Christ/HaMashiach receives his authority and they minister for 3½ years until 75 days before the end of his rule.

> When they finish their testimony, the beast that ascends out of the bottomless pit will make war against them, overcome them, and kill them. Revelation 11:7

However, after 3½ days, which will put them within the 75-day period:

> ... the breath of life from God entered them, and they stood on their feet, and great fear fell on those who saw them. And they heard a loud voice from heaven saying to them, "Come up here." And they ascended to heaven in a cloud, and their enemies saw them. Revelation 11:11

Now it is possible the Post-Tribulation Rapture could very well happen at any time during the literal 3½ days. I say this because in the verse quoted above, it says their enemies saw them. **If their enemies saw them then it would not be the same event for the Believers because Paul says it shall happen in the twinkling of an eye**. I believe the probability is it will happen the day the two witnesses are killed at the beginning of the 75-day period. Nevertheless, perhaps, the rapture event could happen on the same day that the two witnesses are resurrected in that it happens in less than a second. It could perhaps happen a second before or after the two witnesses rise to heaven in a cloud.

However, in Daniel 12:13 we are told whoever waits (reaches) to the 1335th day is blessed. But then, verse seven tells us after a time, times and half a time, 3½ years, all these things shall be finished, which corresponds to the rule of the beast, anti-Christ/HaMashiach. In addition, the book of Daniel tells us the power of the holy people shall be shattered, this would be because of the war of the anti-Christ/HaMashiach against the Believers, Christians and Jews (Revelation 13:7). It has to be when all things are finished we will have reached the end of the time of the authority given to the anti-Christ/HaMashiach. This would include time to arrange for the nations of the world to gather at Armageddon, to annihilate Israel, or as Revelation 16:16 says, "And they gathered them together to the place called in Hebrew, Armageddon." Just before this statement in Rev 16:15, Jesus/Yeshua our Lord announces:

Behold, I am coming as a thief. Blessed is he who watches, and keeps his garments, lest he walk naked and they see his shame. Revelation 16:15

This tells us the Lord will come for His Believers before returning to deal with all the nations at Armageddon and rule the earth with a rod of iron.

CHAPTER EIGHT

MY SUMMATION
OF THE TRI-TRIBULATION RAPTURE

We began this subject of the Tri-Tribulation Rapture with an explanation of my use of the term Rapture. Then I gave definitions of my terms and their use in regard to the Tribulation and Great Tribulation Periods. In addition, an introduction to the three major viewpoints of the rapture, their basic tenants, the controversy that comes from the different interpretations and the use and misuse of scripture was presented. I explained why the Great Tribulation Period was necessary. Then scripturally the precedents for a rapture were given justifying its certainty.

From my review of the literature, each viewpoint was given according to the exegesis of respected authors on each viewpoint of the rapture. **I discussed each in reference to:**

- It's scriptural basis

- It's view of the make-up of the Church

- How long are the Tribulation/Great Tribulation Periods?

- When does the wrath of God begin and how long does it last?

- When does the rapture occur according to the particular viewpoint?

- What do opposing viewpoints have to say regarding the viewpoint?

Concerning the wrath of God, we looked at the language used throughout the Bible, Old and New Testaments that refer to God's wrath. Great tribulation or even tribulation is not universal in its use as a term for the wrath of God in the Bible/Tanakh, Old and New Testaments. Other terms and phrases are used to denote the wrath of God. The phrase "the wrath of God" is found 10 times in the Word of God. Nine times in the New Testament and once in the Old Testament. It is used to indicate God's anger or judgment on non-Believers or the unrighteous. The phrase "the day of the Lord" is used 23 times in the Old and New Testaments to indicate God's anger and judgment upon the disobedient and unbelieving. It is used both in 1 Thessalonians 5:1, 2 referring to the Tribulation Period and in 2 Peter 3:10 regarding God's wrath upon the earth in the last days. However, there is only one instance of the term "the wrath of the Lamb" and it is found in Revelation 6:16.

Why have I presented these statistics? I present them to substantiate that the verses from Revelation 6:12-17 are definitely referring to the wrath of God, which indicates the beginning of the wrath of God. The Tribulation Period begins at verse 12. However, it is not the beginning of the Great Tribulation Period, but it is the beginning of the wrath of God as far as the seven years of the Tribulation Period is concerned.

Some might say Revelation 6:17 marks the beginning of God's wrath. However, comparing the above scriptures with other scriptures, which clearly speak of God's wrath one would have to concede verses 12 through 16 speak of God's wrath also. Therefore, I say the Tribulation Period begins at Revelation 6:12 with the opening of the sixth seal. The period of time from that point, which includes verses 16 and 17 are clearly the wrath of God. The question becomes when does the signing of the treaty occur which signals the beginning of the seven-year tribulation of Daniel 9:27 occur? The signing of the treaty is not mentioned in Revelation chapter 6 nor does it state what length of time these six verses of scripture encompass. As far as how long the wrath of God lasts, I would have to say until all is completed. From the perusal of the scriptures in the book of Revelation, the wrath of God is not complete until chapter 16 verse 20 and the pouring of the last bowl of the wrath of God on the earth. Now how long in years, months and days is guesswork because the start of the wrath of God in chapter 6, verse 12 is not stated definitely, therefore there is no way of knowing exactly. However, **this is my interpretation**, if I am correct in stating the Tribulation Period begins at Revelation 6:12 and it includes the wrath of God then the wrath of God would be seven years.

I gave justification that God will take out or save His people from the wrath, which He will pour out upon those who dwell upon the earth (Revelation 3:7-13). The justification for having three events is "Jesus Christ is the same yesterday, today, and forever" (Hebrews 13:8). Therefore, He will not only take out those who are saved before the Tribulation Period starts but will also take those out who come to salvation within the Tribulation Period, for He is just. Matthew 20:1-16, "The Parable of the

Workers in the Vineyard," **this parable relates how the last as well as the first shall receive the same reward**. His reward regarding the Tribulation Period is the rapture of those who have come to **salvation** whether **before, during or at the end** of the Tribulation Period.

There are three rapture events as stated above. **The first is the Pre-Tribulation Rapture event.** This event must take place before the signature of the prince (the anti-Christ/HaMashiach/the beast) is completed. Mind you, the event can occur any time before the signing of the treaty. The fact I have shown three prominent scriptures supporting there will be a rapture event prior to the wrath of God is sufficient proof the event will take place. The three scripture references quoted in the body of this work are as follows: 1 Thessalonians 1:9, 10; 1 Thessalonians 5:9; and Revelation 3:10.

In reference to the Revelation 3:10 scripture, this is the Lord Himself **dictating** this to the Apostle John. This is not a prophet or scribe receiving by inspiration of Holy Spirit and then, in some cases, writing what he remembers the Lord saying. This is Jesus/Yeshua giving a direct command to the Apostle John to write what the Spirit is saying to the churches. This is God Himself speaking. We must understand the Apostle John was writing about that time in history regarding the specific churches and the Church as a whole. In addition, the churches were also a foreshadowing of the Church as a whole today. The Lord told the Apostle John the characteristics of each of the representative churches they had at that time and those things they who made up the churches needed to overcome in order to achieve everlasting life. Therefore, the Lord was speaking to the future Church through all generations until His return. Each church had those who would overcome. Only one did not have to overcome. Those in that church the Lord will keep from the hour of trial that is to come "upon the whole world." That is the church at Philadelphia. To them he said to "hold fast" to that which they had so "no one" would take their crown. In order to be kept from the hour of trial the most plausible possibility would be the rapture before the Tribulation Period starts. Of course, we cannot limit the Lord to only this solution for the Lord is limitless in possibilities. However, with several scriptures pointing to and supporting a Pre-Tribulation Rapture, we can say with certainty the Pre-Tribulation Rapture will occur. After the Pre-Tribulation event, the signing by the anti-Christ/HaMashiach (Beast) of the seven-year peace treaty of Israel with "many" nations surrounding Israel occurs (Daniel 9:27). The signatory nations most likely will be the Sunni and Shi'ite Islamic nations. The prime goal of Islam is to destroy Israel and there are two primary factions in Islam, the Sunnis and the Shi'ites. The Shi'ites are fundamentally more radical than the Sunnis and would be the most likely not to sign an agreement for peace with Israel. Of course, we can look at how unsuccessful peace negotiations with Israel have been with the Arab nations and the PLO (Palestinian Liberation Organization) since the 1967 war. Why? Because the basic premise of Islam is Israel is not to exist, therefore Islam will not agree to peace on any terms. This is probably the reason the scripture says the prince will sign with many and not all. However, radical Shi'ites despise Sunni Muslims almost as much as they do

Israel, which may cause Sunni nations to sign a "Temporary Peace Treaty" (7 years) with Israel.

Now as far as to when is the year and the day the Pre-Tribulation Rapture event will occur, we can look to the Biblical calendar and with scripture surmise what the possibility **might** be. The Apostle Paul tells us in 1 Corinthians 15:52 we will be changed "in a twinkling of an eye, at the last trumpet." Scripture tells us there is the Feast of Trumpets, Yom Teruah, which occurs on Tishrei one on the Biblical calendar, which is Rosh Hashanah, the civil New Year for Israel. Tishrei is the seventh month on God's calendar (August/September). On this day, God gave commandment to blow trumpets in a series of trumpet blasts of which the last is the loudest and longest. Could this be the day for the Pre-Tribulation Rapture to happen? I believe so. You may say Scripture says we do not know the day or the hour the Lord shall come, Matthew 24:36. I agree. In that regard, The Feast of Trumpets, because of the diaspora of the Jewish nation, Yom Teruah, the Feast of Trumpets, is celebrated on two consecutive days, one for those in Israel and one for those outside of the homeland. Also, in 1 Thessalonians 4:16 the Apostle Paul says the trumpet of God will sound and the rapture will occur. Now as far as the year we can take a cue from some of the Orthodox Rabbis, HaMashiach will come the year after a Shemittah year. We know we are near to the rapture because most of the signs have occurred including the Blood Moon Tetrad (group of four) of the years 5775/76 (2014/15). The Blood Moons (full moons that appear red) occurred on consecutive Passover and Tabernacles feast days with a total solar eclipse in the middle of the four consecutive Blood Moons. So, what does this tell us? We should be ever watchful and occupied with the Lord's business so we do not miss the Rapture. Another point to consider is the Lord was 33 when He resurrected from the grave. Therefore, we may not be quite to the seventh millennium, which we can possibly deduce will be the year of the Second Advent of the Lord. If so, it is probable the year 2033 may be the year of His return. If we deduct seven years then 2026 *"could be"* the year of the Pre-Tribulation Rapture. **You ask if we can be sure. No! Why? Because we are not sure of the year the Lord was born.** Some who have researched the birth of the Lord have said His year of birth could be four to six years before the turn of the century. As a result, we are almost assured of not having the year correct. **Nevertheless, it does give us a *season* of expectation.** Further, if He is returning on a Feast of Teruah the year after a Shemittah year and since 5775 (2015 on the Gregorian calendar) was a Shemittah year then we can determine the next few Shemittah years which are 5782 (2022), 5789 (2029) and 5796 (2036). The last of these is past the year 2033, but I place it there to let the reader know I acknowledge I do not know when the rapture shall occur. **I only want to impress upon the reader we are very near and we should be watchful, take heed and pay attention especially to what is going on with Israel.** My best guess would be if the Lord were born four to six years before the turn of the century then the Shemittah year of 5789 (2029), would be the Shemittah that marks the Lord's Second coming in the year following the Shemittah. Then the seven-year Tribulation Period would start in the year after 5782 (2022) starting with 5783

(2023) on Yom Teruah 1 or 2 with the Pre-Tribulation Rapture. Too many ifs have to be fulfilled to say this is definitely how it is going to happen. What is most important is to be serious about being watchful. I have placed an emphasis on the Feast of Yom Teruah because the Lord resurrected at the Feast of Unleavened Bread/Passover, so it is reasonable to expect the rapture would occur on a Feast Day.

Why do I feel the Pre-Tribulation Rapture is so near at hand? For one, the Blood Moon Tetrad of 2014/15 has occurred with the total solar eclipse in the middle of the four Blood Moons. For me this satisfies the Joel 2:30-32 scripture, which opens the door for the soon return of the Lord. In addition, historically over the past 500 years the Blood Moon Tetrads have been ominous signs for Israel's move toward its destiny. Second, while there have been multitudes coming to salvation there have also been many who have fallen away from their faith in Jesus Christ/Yeshua HaMashiach. Paul says this falling away must happen first. Third, so many nations are aligning themselves against Israel. Fourth, there are nations coming together to form alliances both politically, financially and structurally which points to a one world government. Fifth and not the least of these is the development of the biochip, which is able to be implanted and is being done on the excuse for security, health and informational purposes. Then finally, the Orthodox Jews have in place all they need to reinstitute sacrifice and offerings. Therefore, we see with all these things occurring at the same time there is great pressure spiritually and physically being introduced to bring about the last of the Biblical prophecies that must occur. Besides we see every day the efforts to bring about a treaty with the Arab nations and Israel. We can certainly testify as a whole there is a drastic reduction in the moral code worldwide. Jesus/Yeshua said of His coming, the moral condition of the world would be as in Noah's day.

The second event is the Mid-Tribulation Catching/Away event. After the Pre-Tribulation Rapture we know that there are 7 years (2520 days) until the end or the Tribulation Period. I believe the strongest scripture supporting the Mid-Tribulation event is Revelation 7:9-14. Here John is confessing he does not know who the Saints/Believers are or where they came from and the elder tells him they came out of the Great Tribulation. Therefore, from this exchange we can determine these are different from those the Apostle John saw in Revelation 5:11-13, because they are present before the sixth seal is opened. Therefore, because these are different from those in chapter 5 and we are told they came out of the Great Tribulation then they cannot be Pre-Tribulation Believers. To support this further we read the following scripture:

> Do not fear any of those things which you are about to suffer. Indeed, the devil is about to throw some of you into prison, that you may be tested, and you will have tribulation ten days. Be faithful until death, and I will give you the crown of life. Revelation 2:10

We can see this is the Lord saying to the persecuted church at Smyrna they will have to go into

some tribulation. This also alludes to a portion of the church having to go into a portion of the Tribulation Period.

From the timetable for the Mid-Tribulation Rapture event there is a window of 554 days between the 631st day (the earliest day the middle of the week can occur); and the 1185th day from the beginning of the Tribulation Period; and 75 days before the anti-Christ receives his full power to rule over the one world government.

If we look at our timetable, we will be able to see we can explain all of the scriptures regarding the Mid-Tribulation Rapture event and not violate and yet allow scriptural interpretation for the two other major viewpoints. First, we allow for the occurrence of the Pre-Tribulation Rapture to have taken place. **Second,** because Revelation 6:12-17 describes for us the beginning and escalating wrath of the Lord and yet allows time for the Mid-Tribulation Rapture to occur we can say these verses cover the first 3½ years of the Tribulation Period. As Bill Burns describes in his *"Seven Seals" A Study in Revelation*, regarding the rapture, in which the rolling back of the sky he says is pointing to a doorway for the possibility of the Mid-Tribulation Rapture event to occur (Burns). This is stated in verse 14 before verse 17 the wrath of the Lamb has come. I say this because according to my timetable the Mid-Tribulation Rapture is going to happen before the anti-Christ/anti-HaMashiach actually consolidates his power and control over the one world government. In addition, Revelation 12:6, 14 tells us Israel as a whole is protected for 3½ years. Because the scripture says "the woman was given two wings of a great eagle" (our national bird is the bald eagle) we can say the **United States will be instrumental in protecting Israel through the first 3 ½-year period of time in the Tribulation Period.** Because both verse six and 14 tell us Israel is in a wilderness for 3 ½ years we can surmise the Mid-Tribulation Rapture will be comprised of Christian Believers and just a few Messianic Believers because most of Israel will not yet be ready to receive Yeshua HaMashiach as Messiah.

What we understand is the governments of the world are at relative peace, at least in the Middle East because the treaty (covenant) is in place. It is my belief from the time of the Pre-Tribulation Rapture until the Mid-Tribulation Rapture many of those in the *Church* will have come to Christ/HaMashiach and are prepared for the next event. **The first rapture will have been a mighty wake-up call in the earth** and most if not all who had fallen away will have repented and returned to Jesus Christ/Yeshua HaMashiach. Therefore, the Lord will take out those who are saved to this point so they do not experience any greater tribulation than they have already.

Therefore, the Mid-Tribulation event should take place between the 631st day and the 1185th day. My feeling is it will probably occur on or just before the 1185th day of the Tribulation Period, 75 days before the anti-Christ/HaMashiach assumes full power as ruler of the one world government.

The statement by Our Lord that the days *would* be shortened for the elect's sake is placed at 75 days before the anti-Christ/HaMashiach takes over completely.

Table XI

The Mid-Tribulation Rapture Event
Explained

Mid-point of the 70th Week

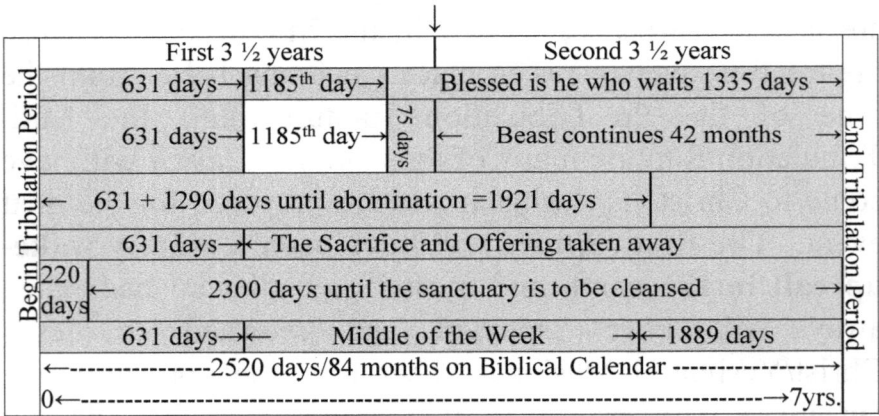

	First 3 ½ years		Second 3 ½ years	
Begin Tribulation Period	631 days→ 1185th day→		Blessed is he who waits 1335 days →	End Tribulation Period
	631 days→ 1185th day→	75 days	← Beast continues 42 months →	
	← 631 + 1290 days until abomination =1921 days →			
	631 days→ ←The Sacrifice and Offering taken away			
	220 days ← 2300 days until the sanctuary is to be cleansed →			
	631 days→ ← Middle of the Week →←1889 days			
	←----------------2520 days/84 months on Biblical Calendar ----------------→			
	0←--→7yrs.			

The 1335 days of Daniel 12:12 is the scripture that sets the Mid-Tribulation Rapture because it is from this point in time the Lord has said for a Believer to endure to be blessed. Therefore, no rapture can occur from this point until 75 days before the end of the Tribulation Period. In addition, the rapture occurring prior to the anti-Christ/HaMashiach gaining complete control allows for keeping the Saints/Believers from the wrath to come in the Great Tribulation. Finally, I am showing the taking away of sacrifice and offering can occur anytime on or after the 631st day until or before the 1889th day and not violate the middle of the week and still be before the abomination of desolation. Therefore, we can put all of the essential ingredients in for the Mid-Tribulation Rapture and not interfere with any scriptures pertaining to the other two rapture events.

Now for the third event, the Post-Tribulation Rapture. The main scriptures are Revelation 14:13-16; Revelation 15:1, 2; Matthew 24:15.

In the Pre-Tribulation Rapture event our bodies will be changed just prior to or at the signing of the seven-year Peace Treaty. The Mid-Tribulation Rapture event would occur before the point the anti-Christ/HaMashiach receives his full authority to govern, which will last for 3½ years. The Jews will be in complete rebellion against the anti-Christ/HaMashiach after the revealing of the abomination of desolation. The abomination of desolation is set up at 1290 days after sacrifice and offerings are taken away which I place at the 631st day. The abomination therefore has to happen no earlier than the 1921st day of the Tribulation Period. Similarly, it is limited to happening before the 75th day before the end of the Tribulation Period because the Post-Tribulation Rapture will occur at that time. In addition, the inference of Matthew 24:15, 16 is there will be a period after the abomination of desolation for people to flee. The abomination of desolation must occur from the 1921st day to before the 2445th day of the Tribulation Period (75 days before the end). That gives us a period of 524 days in which the abomination of desolation can occur. I believe the abomination of desolation is when the anti-Christ/HaMashiach (beast) goes into the Temple and announces he is God, at which time the Orthodox, Conservative and many if not most of the Reformed and secular Jews will not receive him.

The people that come to Christ/HaMashiach during the Great Tribulation, Jew and Gentile will have to try to avoid martyrdom. They will have to endure until the rapture. This will occur 75 days before the end of the reign of the anti-Christ/HaMashiach, which will conclude with the Lord's Second Coming. The Second Coming will also mark the 1335th day from the Mid-Tribulation Rapture. At this point, the anti-Christ/HaMashiach and his government are making the preparations for the final wave of attacks on the Jewish population.

The fact the Lord has given us a glimpse of the 75-day period by saying the person who makes it to the 1335th day will be blessed allows us to give a scenario that will comfortably allow for three rapture events. This is the *KEY* to resolving the *rapture of the Church*.

The most difficult event to resolve historically has been the Post-Tribulation Rapture event. Without the 75-day period at the end of the Great Tribulation Period, apologists (defenders) have had to make the rapture happen on the very last day of the Great Tribulation. That is not the worst of the apology (defense). To make the event work and have the Lord return the same day they have to have the Believers meet the Lord on His descent and return with Him for His Second Advent, which many call the yo-yo effect.

Another disadvantage to this exegesis is the Post-Tribulation event misses the **Marriage Supper of the Lamb** entirely which would deprive these Believers of their rewards and the joy of attending the supper itself.

This would also violate the premise of Hebrews 13:8, "Jesus Christ is the same yesterday, today and forever," and He is not a respecter of persons.

Having this period of 75 days before the Lord returns to rule and reign makes it possible to explain the events without having to deny any scripture, which pertains to the Tribulation Period. We can now place each event in place according to scripture and not violate the other two events.

So, let us put together a scenario of what happens during the Great Tribulation, the second half of the Tribulation Period. The anti-Christ/HaMashiach has been confirmed as the Supreme Ruler of the One World Government after the signing of the 7-year Peace Treaty of Israel and its neighboring Arab nations (Revelation 13:5). The Pre-Tribulation and the Mid-Tribulation rapture events have occurred. He then declares war against all Saints/Believers (Revelation 13:6). This occurs at the mid-point of the Tribulation Period and he is given authority for 42 months (3 ½ years). We notice at this time the two witnesses of Revelation 11:3 have arrived to prophesy and witness for 1260 days (3 ½ years) on the day of the rapture. Through their witness and that of the 144,000, Revelation 7:4; 14:1-5 many Jews and some Gentiles come to Jesus/Yeshua and are saved.

The trial becomes fierce because of the law the anti-Christ/HaMashiach has made that everyone must receive a mark in their flesh (Revelation 13:16).

The witnesses, the 144,000 sealed Israelites, the Bible and the angel preaching the gospel, Revelation 14:4-

8, make it known you must avoid taking the mark (Revelation 14:9, 10).

Table XII

The Post-Tribulation Rapture Event Explained

Mid-point of the 70th Week

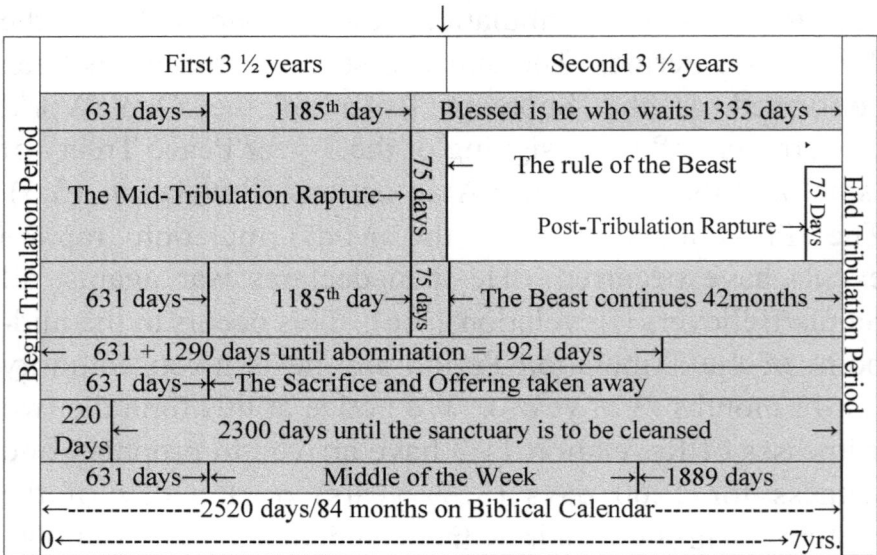

	First 3 ½ years		Second 3 ½ years	
Begin Tribulation Period	631 days→	1185th day→	Blessed is he who waits 1335 days →	End Tribulation Period
	The Mid-Tribulation Rapture→	75 days ←	The rule of the Beast Post-Tribulation Rapture →	75 Days
	631 days→	1185th day→ 75 days	← The Beast continues 42months →	
	← 631 + 1290 days until abomination = 1921 days →			
	631 days→ ←The Sacrifice and Offering taken away			
	220 Days ←	2300 days until the sanctuary is to be cleansed →		
	631 days→ ←	Middle of the Week → ←1889 days		
	←---------------2520 days/84 months on Biblical Calendar----------------→			
	0←--→7yrs.			

Then we come to the premiere scriptures for the Post-Tribulation Rapture:

Then I looked, and behold, a white cloud, and **on the cloud sat One like the Son of Man,** having on His head a golden crown, and in

His hand a sharp sickle. And another angel came out of the temple, crying with a loud voice to Him who sat on the cloud, **"thrust in Your sickle and reap,** for the time has come for You to reap, for the harvest of the earth is ripe." So, He who sat on the cloud thrust in His sickle on the earth, and **the earth was reaped.** Revelation 14:14-16 Emphasis added.

This is the point when the Post-Tribulation event takes place. Jesus/Yeshua is the One who sits on the cloud. He reaps His harvest of souls from the earth. After this, we have the events of the last 75 days, which include the seven bowl or vial judgments of the final wrath of God. We know this because scripture says "After these things" in Revelation 15:5, then the seven last plagues are poured out in Revelation chapter 16. The seven last plagues occur during the last 75 days of the Tribulation Period and allow the Post-Tribulation Saints/Believers to attend the Marriage Supper of the Lamb.

From this point, events follow a more precise chronological order. What occurs after this is **the Lord puts down all rebellion upon the earth by defeating all the kings of the earth led by the beast, the anti-Christ/anti-HaMashiach** (Revelation 19:19). The beast and the false prophet (the second beast) are captured and thrown into the Lake of Fire (Revelation 19:20). Satan is chained up in the Pit for one thousand years (Revelation 20:2-3). The Lord Jesus Christ/Yeshua HaMashiach then sets up rule upon the earth for a millennium, a thousand years (Revelation 20:4).

EPILOGUE

The great significance of *The Tri-Tribulation Rapture of the Church* for us is the Bride of Christ/HaMashiach is the Church, which includes those who shall be raptured. The Church, which is married to Jesus Christ/Yeshua HaMashiach **consists of all of the Believers** who have been saved, none is left out, and therefore **all** shall attend the Marriage Supper of the Lamb. Because there are scriptures that allude to the rewards of the Saints/Believers according to what they have done for Christ/HaMashiach. It is evident the Marriage Supper of the Lamb is the proper place and time for that to occur (1 Corinthians 3:12-15).

I had to carry my subject through the Marriage Supper of the Lamb because it is important to show all Believers, Messianic and Christian, Old and New Testament will be at the Marriage Supper of the Lamb. Revelation 19:7 says, "His wife has made herself ready." This means all who are in Christ are present to be married to Him. Jesus/Yeshua said regarding His Coming:

> Immediately after the tribulation of those days the sun will be darkened, and the moon will not give its light; the stars will fall from heaven, and the powers of the heavens will be shaken. Then the sign of the Son of Man will appear in heaven, and then all the tribes of the earth will mourn, and they will see the Son of Man coming on the clouds of heaven with

power and great glory. And He will send His angels with a great sound of a trumpet, and they will gather together His elect from the four winds, from one end of heaven to the other. Matthew 24:29-31

When we look at the above passage, it is clear it is speaking about after *The Great Tribulation* **for it says what follows is "after the tribulation of those days." It says all who are on the earth will mourn and see Him; these cannot be the Believers, the elect, because we would rejoice to see Him.** Furthermore, the rapture events are instantaneous and no one on earth shall witness the event. For those on earth the only thing they shall witness is a disappearance. The scripture above says a "trumpet" blast will announce the gathering of "His elect from … one end of heaven to the other." If that is the case then all of the Believers must already be in heaven in order to be able to return with Him on their white horses. Question: how did they get into heaven to begin with? The only explanation that fits is either they died in Christ, or they were raptured. If this is so, then the viewpoint of the Post-tributionists the rapture is actually a meeting with the Lord Jesus Christ/Yeshua HaMashiach in the air and returning with Him immediately **cannot** be because they never arrive in heaven and would have missed the Marriage Supper of the Lamb! This is a sequence some refer to as the yo-yo effect, which **in actuality would be a reverse yo-yo effect**. To activate a yo-yo, it is thrown down and it comes right back to the point from which it was thrown. **Well in the traditional Post-Tribulation**

event exegesis those who die in the Lord and those who remain rise to meet the Lord in the air **and instead of going to heaven**, they return immediately to earth to the battle of Armageddon. Instead of going down and then up, they go up and then back down, which would be **the reverse of what happens to a yo-yo**.

We must understand God has given us specific generalities in the books of Daniel, Matthew and Revelation and not the specific times, dates and names of the End-Time events. Therefore, we can be only so complete in unraveling the revelation of Jesus Christ/Yeshua HaMashiach which Father God gave to Him. In fact, John was told not to write some of the things he saw. Daniel was certainly told to close up his book until the time of the end. It is interesting to note our Lord did not give any lengths of time regarding the Tribulation Period during the Olivet Discourse. The lengths of time we were given are found in the book of Daniel and the book of Revelation. This suggests He either gave up some of His divine knowledge during His sojourn in His humanity or at the very least not allowed to give the information at the time. Revelation 1:1 tells us "The Revelation of Jesus Christ, which God gave Him to show His servants – things which must shortly take place." If God the Father gave Jesus Christ/Yeshua HaMashiach a revelation He was to pass on to the Lord's servant, the Apostle John, then this tells us He did not know this while He was on earth in His humanity. Knowing this we narrow the possibilities to a point we will be able to be comforted by what God has put into motion and will carry out until it is finished. We must appreciate He has given a little insight as to what the end of things shall be (Revelation 20-22). Knowing this shall or should give us the stamina to see things through until its conclusion.

Now to say a word regarding the question mentioned by proponents of each viewpoint as to who they are who will be ruled over in the millennium. What we must first understand is the Lord at each rapture event will remove all genuine Believers from the earth. Therefore, after the last rapture there will only be those who have rejected Jesus Christ/Yeshua HaMashiach as Lord, Savior and God. My answer regarding who will be left to enter the millennium is this. When the Lord Jesus Christ/Yeshua HaMashiach returns He will put down all rebellion at Armageddon. He will destroy all of the nation's armies. However, not all people will participate in the battle. There are those who are not of age, are too old or are occupied in other endeavors of life. There will be many left to be subjects in the millennial reign of Jesus Christ/Yeshua HaMashiach.

Jesus/Yeshua said in Matthew 24:36, "But of that day and hour no one knows, not even the angels of heaven, but My Father only." Again, in Acts 1:7, "And He said to them, 'It is not for you to know times or seasons which the Father has put in His own authority.'" This is to say we do not know the exact timing of events. But the Lord did say when the leaves on a fig tree sprout and start to turn green we know summer is near (Matthew 24:32). As we see so many of the prophesied events regarding the last days happen, then we can expect the first rapture event may be very near to occurring.

In developing this exegesis, I have relied as much on Biblical periods of time as on scriptures to give more credibility to when possible occurrence of the rapture events can occur. Yet and still I have pointed out according to scripture the events can occur at any time within a certain window of time. **I believe the Lord has done this to allow any individual seeking Him to exercise his or her *faith* to obtain the prize of everlasting life with Him.**

My hope is the reader has been able to understand my exegesis of *The Tri-Tribulation Rapture of the Church*. The foremost concept the reader should take away from this exegesis is our Lord said He would not leave us orphans but would come to us (John 14:18). What I believe makes this viewpoint the most viable is prior to this exegesis the most disconcerting fact in the other presentations is they offer no hope other than what that particular event could offer. However, with this presentation if we should miss the Pre-Tribulation Rapture event we can be comforted and not despair in knowing there are two other events which will take place in which we have opportunity to meet the Lord in the air and forever be with Him. Besides, I believe the Pre-Tribulation event will be the single greatest evangelistic event the world will ever have because the people of the world will see they need to make the decision to receive Jesus/Yeshua as Lord, Savior and God in order to be in the next event. **The purpose of this presentation is to give hope to those *left behind.***

Hopefully we will all go in the first event, but if not remember this, the Lord Jesus Christ/Yeshua HaMashiach "is the same yesterday, today and forever" (Hebrews 13:8). The Lord will give everyone the same opportunity all the way to the end. Remember, "… But he who endures to the end shall be saved" (Mark 13:13).

I will see you at the Marriage Supper of the Lamb!

In His Love,

Robert L. Dickey, PhD.

BIBLIOGRAPHY

Anthony, Richard. "Answers to Common Questions about Preterism." 22 January 2015. *Ecclesia.* Internet. 22 January 2015. <http://www.ecclesia.org/truth/preterist-questions.html>.

Aprile, Michael. "Evidence of Pre-Tribulation Rapture." 3 April 2007. *The Utmost Way Magazine.* Internet. 30 November 2011. <http://utmost-way.com/prophecy/evidence-of-pre-tribulation-rapture>.

Archer, Jr., Gleason L. "THE CASE FOR THE MID-SEVENTIETH-WEEK RAPTURE POSITION." Archer, Jr., Gleason L. . . . [et. al.]. *THREE VIEWS ON THE RAPTURE: PRE-, MID-, OR POST-TRIBULATION.* Ed. Jr., Gleason L. and Stanley N. Gundry Archer. Grand Rapids: Zondervan, 1996. 268. Book.

Armstrong, Roger. *The Second Coming of Christ.* 3 March 2007. Internet. 12 February 2012. <http://post-triborpre-trib.blogspot.com>.

Arnold, William, III. *The Post-Tribulation Rapture.* William Arnold III, 1999. Internet. 12 February 2012. <http://www.onenesspentecostal.com/post/link2.htm>

Baxter, Irvin. "The Second Coming Pt 1." *The End of the Age.* Prod. Irvin Baxter. Costa Mesa: End Time Ministry, 31 March 2012. Internet. 31 March 2012. <http://www.endtime.com>.

—. "The Second Coming Pt 2." *The End of the Age.* Prod. Baxter Irvin. Costa Mesa: Trinity Broadcasting

Network, 16 May 2012. Internet. 16 May 2012. <http://www.endtime.com>.

Burns, Bill. "Seven Seals." *A Study in Revelation*. Vol. Disc 5. Prod. Bill Burns. Kremmling, n.d. CD. <www.resources@ft111.com>.

Combs, William W. "IS APOSTASIA IN 2 THESSALONIANS 2:3 A REFERENCE TO THE RAPTURE?" Fall 1998. *DBTS JOURNAL*. Internet. 8 February 2015. <https://www.dbts.edu/journals/>.

Dennis, Todd. "Seventy Weeks of Daniel." 25 January 2015. *Ecclesia*. Internet. 25 January 2015. <http://www.ecclesia.org>.

Dr. Reagan, David R. "The Pre-Wrath Rapture: Is there any validity to this concept?" 1996-2016. *Lamb & Lion Ministries*. Internet. 22 January 2016. <http://www.lamblion.com/articles/articles_rapture10.php>.

"End Times Made Easy . . . and Complete." 1 May 2012. *Daniel 11: God's Timeline*. Internet. 11 February 2015. <http://daniel11truth.com/index.htm>.

Feinberg, Paul D. "THE CASE FOR THE PRETRIBULATION RAPTURE POSITION." Archer, Gleason L. Jr., Stanley N. Gundry . . . [et. Al.]: Dennis L. Okholm & Timothy R. Phillips, eds. *THREE VIEWS ON THE RAPTURE: PRE-, MID-, OR POST-TRIBULATION*. Ed. Jr. and Stanley N. Gundry Gleason L. Archer. Grand Rapids: Zondervan, 1996. 268. Book.

Finley, Gavin, M.D. "A Chart of the 70th Week of Daniel." November 2000. *End-Time Pilgrim*. Internet.

25 April 2015.
<http://www.endtimepilgrim.org/chart2.htm>.

—. "The Coming Year of Jubilee." November 2000. *End-Time Pilgrim.* Internet. 26 April 2015.
<http://www.endtimepilgrim.org/index.htm>.

—. "The Day of the Lord." November 2000. *End-Time Pilgrim.* Internet. 26 April 2015.
<http://www.endtimepilgrim.org/dotl.htm>.

—. "The Post-Tribulation Rapture." November 2000. *End-Time Pilgrim.* Internet. 4 April 2015.
<http://endtimepilgrim.org/posttribrap.htm>.

Hoekema, Anthony. "Amillenialism: A Brief Sketch of Amillennial Eschatology/Future 5." 22 January 2015. *The Highway: Calvinism and the Reformed Faith.* Internet. 22 January 2015. <http://www.the-highway.com>.

—. "Amillennialism: A Brief Sketch of Amillennialial Eschatology/Inaugurated 2." 22 January 2015. *The Highway: and the Reformed Faith.* Internet. 22 January 2015. <http://www.the-higway.com>.

Houdmann, S. Michael, CEO. *Is the last trumpet of 1 Thessalonians 4 the same as seventh trumpet of Revelation?* February 2002. Internet. 5 February 2015. <http://www.gotquestions.org/last-trumpet.html>.

Kavanaugh, Ellen. "Understanding the Post-Tribulation Rapture." 1997-2013. *Light of Mashiach.* Internet. 15 April 2015. <http://www.lightofmashiach.org>.

—. "Yom Teruah: Day Of The Shofar Blasts." 1997 - 2013. *Light of Mashiach!* Internet. 9 June 2015.

<http://www.lightofmashiach.org/post_trib_rapture.htm
l>.

Kelley, Jack. "Defending the Pre-Trib Rapture (Again)."
2006. *Grace Through Faith.* Internet. 3 December
2011. <http://gracethrufaith.com/ikvot-
hamashiach/defending-the-pre-trib-rapture-again/>.

Kinsella, Jack. "The Mid-Tribulational View: The Rapture
of the Church - Part Three." n.d. *Everlasting Life
Ministries.* Internet. 11 February 2015.
<http://www.everlastinglifeministries.com/rapture/rap_
mid_trib.asp>.

Koenig, Don. "Proofs for pretribulation Rapture." n.d. *The
Prophetic Years.* Internet. 12 February 2012.
<http://www.thepropheticyears.com/comments/featured
_bible_prophecy_teachings_by_don_koenig.htm>.

Larkin, Clarence. *Dispensational Truth.* 1920. Internet. 19
January 2015. <http://www.preservedwords.com>.

Lemke, Steve W. "THE BIBLICAL CASE FOR MID-
TRIBULATIONALISM." n.d. *New Oreans Baptist
Theological Seminary.* Internet. 4 February 2015.
<http://www.nobts.edu/faculty/itor/lemkesw//personal/
midtribulationism.html>.

Moo, Douglas J. "THE CASE FOR THE
POSTTRIBULATION RAPTURE POSITION."
Archer, Gleason L., Jr. . . . et al. *THREE VIEWS ON
THE RAPTURE: PRE-, MID-, OR POST-
TRIBULATION.* Ed. Jr. and Stanley N. Gundry Gleason
L. Archer. Grand Rapids: Zondervan, 1996. 268. Book.

NTEB. "The Pre-tribulation Rapture of the Church
Explained: Understanding the Time of the Pre-

tribulation Rapture through End Times Bible Prophecy." 2009. *Now The End Begins.* Internet. 19 February 2012. <http://nowtheendbegins.com>.

Reagan, David R. "The Rapture." n.d. *Rapture Forums.* Internet. 12 February 2015. <http://www.raptureforums.com/Rapture/therapture.cfm>.

Reiter, Richard R. "A HISTORY OF THE DEVELOPMENT OF THE RAPTURE POSITIONS." Archer, Gleason L. Jr. . . . [et. Al.]. *THREE VIEWS ON THE RATURE: PRE-, MID-, OR POST-TRIBULATION.* Ed. Jr. and Stanley N. Gundry Gleason L. Archer. Grand Rapids: Zondervan, 1996. 268. Book.

Rosemary1947. "50 Evidences for the Pre-Trib Rapture." 2000. *Christian Discussions MSN.* Internet. 12 February 2012.

Rosenthal, Marvin J. "The Question of Chronology." *Zion's Fire* Mar/Apr 2011: 3. Internet. 2 February 2015. <http://www.zionshope.org/index.aspx>.

Roth, Sid. *The Incomplete Church.* Shippensbburg: Destiny Image Publishers, Inc., 2007. Book.

Schang, Chris. "What is the Mid-Tribulation Rapture Theory?" 2007-2015. *Rapture Forums.* Internet. 13 February 2015. <http://www.raptureforums.com/Rapture/whatisthemidtribulationrapture.cfm>.

Schwertley, Brian M. "Is The Pre-Tribulation Rapture Biblical?" 1999. *Reformed Online.* Internet. 12 February 2012.

<http://www.reformedonline.com/uploads/1/5/0/3/1503 0584/is_the_pretribulation_rapture_biblical.pdf>.

Simmons, Kurt M. "What Is Preterism?" 22 January 2015. *Preterist Central.* Internet. 22 January 2015. <http://www.preteristcentral.com>.

Stanton, Gerald. "Kept From The Hour." n.d. *Rapture Forums.* Internet. 12 February 2015. <www.raptureforums.com/geraldstanton>.

Stern, David. *The Complete Jewish Bible.* Clarkesville: Messianic Jewish Publishers, 1998. Book.

Stewart, David J. "The Pretribulation Rapture." n.d. *Jesus is Savior.* Internet. 12 February 2012. <http://www.jesus-is-savior.com/Believer's%20Corner/pretribulation_rapture .htm>.

Stone, Perry. "Part 2 The Book of Remembrance and The Parables." *The Book of Remembrance.* Vol. Disc 2. Prod. Perry Stone. Cleveland: Voice of Evangelism, 2007. CD. <www.perrystone.org>.

Strandberg, Todd. "Defending the Pre-Trib Rapture." n.d. *Rapture Ready.* Internet. 4 December 2011. <http://www.raptureready.com/rr-pre-trib-rapture.html>.

—. "The Pre-Tribulation Rapture." 12 February 2012. *Rapture Ready.* Internet. 12 February 2012. <http://www.raptureready.com>.

Totten, M.Div., Rhett. *The Church and the Post-Tribulation Rapture.* 2009. Internet. 4 June 2015. <http://worldview3.50webs.com/2raptureindex.html>.

Vaterhaus, Gary. "Millennial and Rapture Positions." n.d. *Sola Scriptura Preents.* Internet. 4 March 2015. <www.solagroup.org>.

Winston, Bill. "Pawn Shop of Satan." *Fellowship of Inner City Ministers*. Ed. None. Los Angeles: Live, 2012. Live. Speaker.

About the Author

Robert L. Dickey, D.D.S., D.Min., Ph.D. is an apostle, Bible Prophecy End-Time Teacher and conference speaker. He is an author whose books give revelation and understanding of these "Last Days." In addition, one of his ministry assignments in the marketplace is to establish Christian dental and health centers. He has seen signs and wonders, healings and lives changed through the power of God. Dr. Robert holds a Doctor of Philosophy in Religious Studies and a Doctor of Ministry from FICU in Merced, California and a Doctor of Dental Surgery. He along with his wife, Audrey L. Dickey, PhD received a vision to establish an international apostolic-prophetic ministry. They are the founders and CEO's of Christian Love Glory International Center as well as the apostles and founders of Christian Love Fellowship Church, Inc. This Fivefold multi-cultural ministry includes covenant restoration of the One New Man and will oversee designated marketplace businesses. Drs. Robert and Audrey Dickey have five children and make their home in Los Angeles, California.

To Contact the Author:

Dr. Robert L. Dickey
P. O. Box 48288
Los Angeles, CA 90048

www.robertandaudreydickeyministries.org